Ideological Training in Communist Education: A Case Study of Romania

Martin J. Croghan
School of Education
Northwestern University

Penelope P. Croghan
Northwestern University

D0171179

University Press of America™

Library of Congress Catalog Card Number: 79-47986

CONTENTS

LIST OF FIGURES

PREFACE

It is frequently forgotten that the drive behind the compulsory education movement in the last century was motivated by the desire to shape a new geographical union into a national unit. We tend nowadays to disregard the compulsory, and focus on the more liberal aspect of the right of all citizens to an education. And unfortunately for our political understanding of systems of education, we are inclined to see the function of education in purely educational terms. People do acquire skills such as reading, writing and computing in school. It is equally true, but not equally obvious, that the function of education is political: to assimilate the future citizens into a condition where they are controlled.

The degree of control and the expected obedience differs from society to society, and from era to era within the same society. In this volume the ideological training in a Communist society is examined. The situation is classical. Romania in its internal politics follows the traditional pattern of high centralization and control, with little or no pluralism.

It is hoped that the presentation in the present volume will lead to an examination in detail of the politicization process within our own school systems. Awareness and further knowledge should not unduly disturb us.

Martin Croghan was primarily responsible for the field work and Penelope Croghan for the coordination and final reporting.

An intellectual debt of long standing to Howie Becker is happily acknowledged, but expecially in the area of the mode of the reporting of research material. He bears no responsibility however for the content of the book. A debt of twenty years is also publicly acknowledged: to the demanding Philosophy Department of the University of Dublin.

CHAPTER I

METHODOLOGY AND DESIGN OF THE STUDY

In this chapter, I will deal with the background to the research, the main aspects of the methodology, the design and the validity of the study.

Part I: Background
Section 1: Conceptualization

When I first went to Romania as a lecturer in the department of Germanic languages at Bucharest University, in 1971, I had an extensive knowledge of Marxism and the Marxist tradition. I had read the usual works on Communism by Fainsod, Deutscher, Koestler, Friedrich, Brzezinski, Djilas and some works that dealt specifically with Romania by Ionescu and Fischer-Galati. Conceptually I would have subscribed to the assumption accepted by political scientists such as Almond and Bingham Powell, Laski, de Jouvenel,[1] and by such anthropologists as Mead, Fromm and Honigmann,[2] that: in every society there must be a common moral language for the continuation of power, if a society is to endure;[3] or in anthropological terms, that "a nuclear character structure must be shared 'by most members of the same culture' in order for the culture to continue; socialization must make people want to act as they have to act".[4]

My initial contact with the constant emphasis on ideology in Romania did nothing to change my assumption that a nuclear character structure must be shared by the majority of the members of a culture. Bertram D. Wolfe sums up the emphasis on ideology in a communist state by saying ideology is contained in:

. . . all the modes of expression, communication, criticism, thought, feeling, all

1

cheers and boos, all love and hate, all paper, ink, type, loudspeakers, microphones,
cameras, cinemas, montage and cutting rooms,
theaters, walls, schools, churches, street-
corners, all books, magazines, newspapers,
leaflets, caricatures, pulpits, chairs, lec-
terns, meeting halls, all import and export
of ideas . . . .[5]

The first few months of being exposed to the
constant ideological training in Romania functioned as further reinforcement for me that the
Mead assumption about society and education in
society, as being the 'replication of uniformity',
was a very reasonable and productive assumption
in studying any society.[6] The research over the
next five years that changed this assumption was
very uncomfortable intellectually. The research
made it impossible for me to continue with the
assumption that a high amount of uniformity is
necessary for the very existence of society, although the assumption has a certain attractiveness
in its superficial logic. Pluralism or the 'organization of diversity'[7] became the substitute
assumption: that a sharing of attitudes, motives
and values is not a sine qua non for the functioning of an institution or a society.

It is interesting that the assumption outlined above, as held by both political scientists
and anthropologists, is similar to the driving
force behind many Communist societies. In Romania, communism entails not only the changing of
ownership or social control by nationalization,
but the changing of human nature itself, in the
creation of 'the new Socialist man'. Communism
will never succeed unless there is a common moral
language, a nuclear communist character that is
shared by all. The new generation must be social-
ized to want to act for the good of the communist
state, to want to act as they have to act.[8]

Some writers on communist affairs maintain
that Communist leaders make a distinction between
the elite and the masses, with politics the con-

cern for the apparat elite and social and economic affairs the concern for the masses.[9] Gilberg
Trond, in his <u>Modernization in Romania since
World War II</u>, states that in some of the Eastern
European countries "the regime seems to have re-
conciled itself to the continuation of ideological lethargy and a citizens' morality that is
less than the new ethics".[10] Janos Kadar in Hungary has stated that the bourgeoisie can exist in
a Communist state as long as they do not work a-
gainst the socialist system.[11] In Romania this
is not the case.

Romania has gotten a lot of attention from
the scholars and journalists since the sixties because it plays the 'wild-card' role in the so-
called iron curtain bloc. But this has not meant
tolerating a passive acceptance of communist ideology. Romania, especially since the advent of
the present political leader in 1965, Nicolae
Ceausescu, emphasizes the holistic nature of social development and modernization. It is not
enough to give passive assent to the regime by
not opposing it. There can be no progress unless
the consciousness of the citizen, the motives,
the attitudes, the values are also communist.
One professor who is also an academician, said to
me in an interview:

> You will be very confused unless you understand
> that if a choice has to be made between the
> politic and the economic, Ceausescu will choose
> the politic; the economic will wait but there
> can be no compromise with the politic.[12]

The first year of my research coincided with
the preparation for the National Party Congress
of the Romanian Communist Party in 1972. The
continual message of the Communist Party newspaper, <u>Scinteia</u>, in the summer of 1972 was reflected
by the message on a wall poster in a school: "Socialism in heart and soul. All united in one
spirit behind Ceausescu on the road to Communism".[13] A campaign in the media, advocating devotion and dedication to socialism and communism,

3

was in full swing in the fall of 1971, preparing for the Congress in 1972. In Romania, socialization through the school system aims at producing conscientious 'socialists' and 'communists'. This goal is a primary objective of the leader of the country. The use of the school to create the new socialist man is the consistent and serious intention of the rulers.

Section 2: Change in Research Orientation

My research in Romania changed directions during the five year period. At first, I intended to examine the teaching of nationalism in the schools of Romania. In the climate after the invasion of Prague by the Soviet troops in 1968, it seemed likely that Communism was finished as an international movement based on a mutually accepted ideology. Writers had already been examining the Sino-Soviet split using a nationalistic framework. I wanted to study the teaching of nationalism in the Romanian schools, in order to identify the conflicts of a nationalistic ideology and an ideology of a Marxian nature that is strongly international, at least in reference to Socialist nations.[14] After a brief period of observation, I realized that nationalism is to some extent given a Marxian base, and communism in Romania is, to some extent, indigenous to Romania.

Ceausescu's main political views represent an original blend of traditional Marxism-Leninism, Romanian nationalism, and a form of populism. The General Secretary is a firm believer in the perfectability of man, and many of his writings are strongly reminiscent of the early Marx, with heavy emphasis on individual emancipation through the collective achievements of society. . . . Man is a social animal who can only reach his highest level through interaction with others.[15]

In the summer of 1971, and continuing through the fall of the same year when I started my research, there began in Romania the cultural revolution or,

4

as it is now referred to in the non-official literature on Romania, the "Mini-Cultural Revolution".[16] The implications for me in the first
six months of research were that I realized that
seeking a nationalist/communist antithesis would
be wasted effort. I changed the orientation of
the research.

I then decided to concentrate on research
that would result in a descriptive analysis of
the content and mode of ideological instruction
in schools from Kindergarten through University.
I felt early on there was an important advantage
to looking at the whole process of the ideological
training. I personally was involved in the final
stage of the person's training in the school system. I wanted to see the genesis of the training
which produced the individual with whom I was
dealing with on a day to day basis. I rejected
the term 'socialization', and the conceptualization underlying the term, because it seems to en-
tail an actual process of personal change. Such
a definition would seem to prejudice the research
I was attempting. For this reason I chose the
more neutral phrase 'ideological training', which
is neutral in the sense that it does not say anything about the efficacy of the training itself.

I was also interested in the question of the
efficacy of communist ideological training. I
soon realized that the anterior question had to be
examined first: what in fact is ideological
training in the communist state of Romania? I
soon realized that sometimes the mode of the
training becomes a significant item. For example,
one of the ways of training students in the ideologically important value of 'work' and 'worker'
is to expose them to a complex set of work engagements. For this reason I chose the term 'training' rather than the scholastic-sounding 'instruction'. The intention in the training is not
simply intellectual understanding, but also com-
mitment, on an intellectual, emotional and physical level.

5

I did not approach the research with a set of models. I left myself open to what I would find. Despite the proliferation of literature on Communism and Communist education, there is little detailed information on the mode and content of the ideological training in Communist societies. I looked on my task as primarily an attempt to study and describe the ideological training in the schools in Romania. Questions of a comparative nature and questions of a more speculative nature, are questions that are posterior to my research, which was essentially field research.

Section 3: Personal Attitude towards Research & Communism

Before dealing with the methods used in field work in more detail, I want to address the question of whether my research is value-free. I would like to be able to say it is, categorically. However it is important to state my own political position. I am not a communist. In general, I favor minimum government control, but advocate government intervention periodically if the basics of life are not guaranteed. Active anti-communism is not a preoccupation of mine however for many reasons, but principally, because in general, I am not very happy intellectually with the current nominalism with regard to the term 'communism'. My purpose in the research is not to criticize Romania or Romanians or the Romanian system of education or communism, however communism may be defined.

Very early in my research I realized it would be presumptuous of me to assume that I knew what, for example, Romanian communism as an ideology is. Comparative communist politics at present and for some time now since the rejection of totalitarianism as the generally acceptable model,[17] is at best confused, with the only consensus being the need for a model.[18] A major problem is there is a paucity of scientific information about what communism is. There is a presumption that we know what communism is. In the final chapter, I will

come back to the problem of trying to say at least
partially, what communism is in Romania, based on
the report of the ideological training in the
school system. The treatment however will be illustrative and existentialist, not essentialist.

Little is known about the functioning of the
so-called communist states individually to make
at present a comparative model that would be anything other than superficial. To compare X and Y
demands a thorough knowledge of X and Y individually, a more thorough knowledge than if X or Y is
examined separately.

Part II: Methodology
Section 1: General Approach

In general it can be said that the philosophy
behind my research methodology is that outlined in
Buford H. Junker's Field Work: An Introduction to
the Social Sciences.[19] Everett C. Hughes in his
introduction to this volume defines field work as
the observation of people in situ; "finding them
where they are, staying with them in some role
which, while acceptable to them, will allow both
intimate observation of certain parts of their
behavior, and reporting it in ways useful to social science but not harmful to those observed."[20]
Junker himself elaborates early in the same work
by adding that field work observes, records, and
reports "the behavior of living people in contemporary situations with no intention of changing
them or their situations, in any direct way, and
with, rather, every intention of avoiding distur-
bance to their natural activities".[21]

In the section of this chapter dealing with
the design of the study, little information will
be given about the schools where I did research
that could identify them. Individuals will be
identified only by profession. I did research in
more schools than I am reporting on now, which
will help in lessening the possibility of distur-
bance to those studied. Being careful about anonymity has made the reporting of the study tortu-

ous. However, though the anonymity of the reporting may sometimes annoy, I am hoping that as Howard Becker says in his essay on Problems in Publication of Field Studies, that I "know whether the suffering will in any sense be proportional to gains science may expect from publication of his findings".[22] I think I do know the situation in Romania. I have also consulted a significant number of Romanians who were very positive about the reporting. It may seem presumptuous to talk about my contribution to 'science' in reporting my research, but factual knowledge resulting from extended field work is scarce in the area of communist education, which consists for the most part in official literature[23] or visitation literature.[24]

I did not set out in the beginning of the research with a formulated hypothesis or set of hypotheses. Keeping to observation, without a defined theory, hypothesis or model was disturbing at first. But as I progressed in the research I became more and more convinced that the general observation and description must come first. Reading the literature on communist studies, en passant with the research, also helped me feel more comfortable with the idea that the general field-work must come before specialized analysis. For example, the lack of valid data in Milton C. Lodge's Soviet Elite Attitudes since Stalin[25] made Lodge's analysis premature, if not totally invalid. The work however, enjoyed great success. It had an aura of scientific method. It computerized 24,000 paragraphs from Soviet journals, but it never asked if any of the paragraphs were valid indicators of real attitude. The hypothesis determined the data, but the data were inadequate to substantiate the hypothesis that since Stalin there is greater participation in the political process by the intellectual or specialist elite.

Section 2: Linguistic Aspects of the Methodology

I was not dependent in my observation and interviews, on an officially selected interpreter or

8

translator. I have a fluent knowledge of Romanian. Sometimes I used English in the interviewing with people who speak fluent English, because they expected me to speak English with them; sometimes I spoke French with older Professors, who felt more comfortable talking with a foreigner in a language other than Romanian; sometimes the interview was bilingual, starting in English or French and then going into Romanian, as the interviewee became more comfortable. But generally the language in the interviewing was Romanian. Unless otherwise stated, all translations from French and Romanian are my own.

Using Romanian is an important factor in the methodology of my research. Firstly, I was not risking the potential mistranslations and misinterpretations that can happen with any interpreter or translator. Mistranslations can happen unintentionally because of the lack of ability of the interpreter or translator, or, the lack of equivalents in the two languages. Mistranslations can be intentional if the translator or interpreter does not want to interpret or translate accurately for some reason or other. For example, because of the Government regulations in Romania about relationships of Romanians with foreigners,[26] an interpreter becomes an official person, with certain obligations about the necessity of reporting to authorities on what was said and observed. The government regulation can cause mistranslation if the translator feels that what is to be translated is not for foreign ears, for example. Another example is one told me by interpreters and translators that I had in a special class: that they often deliberately misinterpret from Romanian into English for example, because they feel embarrassed translating something they are accustomed to in Romanian,[27] but which sounds ridiculous to them in English.

One of the consequences of Romanian sensitivity about patriotism was that the interpreters and translators said they did not want Westerners laughing at Romania. So they sometimes deliber-

9

ately misinterpreted when they felt that if an
authentic translation were given Romania would
appear in a naive light. This applied to patriotic statements or chauvinistic statements in Romanian, as well as political statements. That
these matters were told to me is significant in
that I was exempted from the category of Western-
er, because I knew the language and the sociocultural situation. This was true with my interviews in general. It was felt that I would not
laugh at Romania because I understood the situation, and knew the limits of the available
choices. Almost all of the university students in
the translation group referred to Romania as being
looked down on by westerners. That Romanians are
called the 'gypsy socialists' by the Slavic members of the Eastern European bloc was also referred to. The translators would be inclined to
mistranslate to present Romania in a better light.

If one has an interpreter or a translator,
one is always being potentially observed oneself.
This becomes important when dealing with other
people, because they are no longer talking to you,
but to a third person that they do not know and,
hence may not trust. For methodological reasons,
based on extensive experience, I assumed one Romanian does not trust another unless they know
each other well. If they trust each other, this
fact will be communicated to you. If one already
has a trust relationship with a person or group,
an interpreter who is not trusted can impede the
observation or interview.

Using Romanian is also an important part of
the methodology for a complex linguistic reason.
Romanian is a language which ranges from the very
formal to the very informal, with quite distinct
stages between these two poles. The pronominal
structure in Romanian for example is more complex
than in French, German or even Spanish. This
prenominal structure is reflective of the intimacy
and trust relationship, the social relationship
between two people, the class differences or the
sex differences. The pronominal structure has im-

portant implications for interviewing. If you
interview someone, you are usually interested in
their personal knowledge of, or attitude toward a
particular item. Revealing attitude is usually a
private or intimate act. The State Secrets Act
of Romania covers everything that is not officially published. All public activities are Party
or State activities; criticism of public activities is discouraged.[28] It would be very difficult
to interview people about ideology unless one
wanted to hear only what is in the Party newspaper, Scinteia, if one were to remain on a very
formal level linguistically. Developing a relationship to the stage where an interview about attitudes can take place would be very restricting
with regard to time and number of people interviewed, if one started on a formal language basis.

    I found as a foreigner that I was not bound
by the linguistic strictures that demand the use
of formal Romanian in the beginning of the relationship. I would ask permission to use the
'intimate' forms of the language because my knowledge of colloquial Romanian was better in the beginning than my knowledge of formal Romanian.
Most Romanians that I met seemed to be very amused
and rather flattered, that a foreigner knew colloquial Romanian and Bucharest slang which is the
code used by many male intellectuals and younger
females. For example, telling jokes, especially
'political' jokes, is a significant portion of
social interaction and being able to participate
in this section of the daily life was important
if one were to be accepted as a genuine participator. It was for this reason that I concentrated
in the very beginning on acquiring as perfect a
competence as possible in colloquial Romanian.
That I spoke colloquial Romanian made the interview situation a normal life-situation, where attitudes and reactions could be freely expressed.
Otherwise the situation would have been stilted
making the participation and the interviews arti-
ficial.[29]

    Knowledge of the language was also important

11

because the language code used often served as a clue in the observation and interviewing to determine the role played. The code-clues can be syntactic which are often lost in translation into English because compared to Romanian, English is, for example, lacking in second person pronominal and verbal indicators of social grading. Romanian has four forms in the second person pronominal to the English one. Lexis can be also an indicator of role behavior. The role-determining aspects of a particular lexical code use can be easily lost in translation.^{30} Romania has now been under communist rule for more than thirty years. The political situation has developed a linguistic code which can be easily missed in translation into English especially because the English language belongs to cultures that are dissimilar in political philosophy and structures, so that even though a term or expression may seem to have a literal translation from Romanian into English, the semantic properties of the expression can be quite different. For example, the terms 'work'/'worker' in Romanian have semantic properties with political bases that are usually absent in English. In the Romanian of today, 'work' is a key concept of contemporary Romanian ideology.

It is important for me also to have a thorough knowledge of Romanian to distinguish a trust group from a non-trust group whenever I wanted to interview people in groups. In a social setting, if the group present was not a trust group and there was no opportunity to withdraw to a private space, then it was signalled to me that the conversation was to be kept to neutral affairs. A thorough knowledge of Romanian is necessary to be able to pick up the clues, linguistic and paralinguistic that signal a non-trust situation. A linguistic competence in the language was also necessary to discern stock answers. The same applied to interpreting written Romanian, in newspapers, periodicals, directives and speeches. In the first two years, I frequently solicited help in developing my own competence in the interpretation of speeches and written Romanian. In newspapers in Romania, articles often have different semantic levels with unstated implications that can only be understood by the initiated. For example, a proposition that has a surface structure of a statement of fact may semantically be a criticism, an exhortation or a warning.

Section 3: Two Stages in the Research

There are two somewhat distinct stages in the research. The first stage was to give me general exposure to the educational system and to society in general. Research into the historical background of the ideological training was also done in the first stage. In the second stage, the research was focussed on specific aspects of the ideological training in the schools.

Stage 1: 1971-1973
(A): The Educational System in General

I visited a wide range of schools from K-University. My purpose in this was to orient myself in a practical way to the school system in general, looking at academic, ideological, social, administrative and recreational aspects of the schools. For example, I used the initial two year period of interviewing to ask about teachers' salaries, in-service training, teacher mobility, class preparation, private teaching, time spent at different kinds of meetings, time spent with students outside formal classroom activities, family and social background of faculty and students, grading and mobility of students and historical background. The general visitation of the schools enabled me to choose the particular institutions for the focal and secondary units of research that will be outlined in Part 3 of this chapter. During this period also, I began to learn about the relationship of the school with the Party and State organs and the Unions.

(B): Orientation to Society

One of the important insights for me in the

13

first stage of the research was the changes of
emphasis in the ideological training. Seeking
hypotheses to account for these changes forced me
into the position of becoming a student of the
whole society. As a nation where there is a
structure of government and societal control that
is centralized, Romania can use all the available
means in the whole society to further ideological
training and support for the regime. The question
in accounting for the changes in emphasis in the
ideological training in the schools was: does
what is happening in the schools reflect what is
happening to the country, both internally and in
its external relations? Seeking an answer to this
question involved giving attention to the whole
society: to the media which can only be official;
to the theater, music, the arts, films (both Romanian and foreign). It also involved paying
attention to the word-of-mouth news, which sometimes was sheer gossip, but sometimes was important in explaining ideological changes of emphasis. Chapter II deals with certain aspects of
Romania that are necessary as background for a
further understanding of the ideological training
in the schools.

(C): The Historical Perspective

In the early interviews, many of the teachers
and professors explained the present in terms of
the past. The present ideological training was
compared to the training in the past; certain
items in the contemporary training were given
their historical reference. The media and normal
social intercourse had continual reference to the
past. I decided that I would have to study the
Romanian preoccupation with their past if I was
going to understand the training in the schools.
The result of the study becomes Chapter 3 of this
report. In interviewing about the past, I sought
a consensus about the past, not a purely historical perspective. My knowledge about the past also gave me credibility in later stages of the research.

Stage 2: 1973-1976

I give the dates for the two stages of research as rough indicators. In the second stage, I continued with my attention to the whole of society, and to some extent, with the historical perspective.

But it was in the second stage that I started to organize the analysis, looking at specific hypotheses more closely, to introduce order into the investigation and coherence into the research results. While the first period of the research was devoted in the main to my education, I also relied in the second period of the research on Romanians to guide the detail of the research, taking hints from them about what to look at and why. Some of the people I was interviewing were empirical scientists who in part became my mentors. In general, I suggested that I was interested in a particular area, such as productive or patriotic work for students. Then my mentors advised me what to look at in detail, where and why. The general initiative had to come from me because generally, although Romanians are very aware of the ideological training, they look on the training in the school and the media in a passive way, as external to themselves, as something over which they have no control. An official in the Ministry of Education who was responsible for the planning and writing of text-books containing ideological material, said to me in interview: "What can we do? That's the way it is. A man does what he has to do. It's like an old woman baking a cake. Our writers put in a handful of this, a handful of that, every four or five pages. Then the text-book may get published."[31]

I was, in general, the instigator of the questioning. As an outsider I was able to pursue a question that I was particularly conscious of, for precisely the reason that I was an outsider. I was interested in the ideological training as a whole. Romanians did not regard the training as a unit; they tended to isolate what they regarded

15

as the communist part of the training from the rest of the ideological training.

Particularly in the second stage of the research, I tried: (a) to identify the source of the ideological behavior; (b) to analyze the expectations in the respective ideological role playing among students, teachers, and professors; (c) to analyze the content and mode of the ideological training and behavior in the context of time, place and grouping. The second stage of the research was focussed then on establishing the flow pattern of the ideological training and behavior, using the following framework:

Content

Source   Target

Mode

Behavioral expectation was the key concept in trying to establish the flow pattern.

In the research I tried to avoid looking at purpose but it was continually mentioned in interviews, whether solicited or not. I had decided to avoid looking at purpose for two reasons. Firstly, the notion of purpose is an ambiguous one. It can refer to the intention of the person, or the purpose of the action itself. For example, my purpose in reprimanding someone can be intended to help that person positively; the reprimanding itself may be of such a kind that it induces depression. Secondly, purpose, in either of the two senses that I have outlined, is difficult to identify scientifically because of its inaccessibility and complexity. The analysis of purpose belongs to psychology and psychiatry because intended purpose may be either conscious or subconscious. The conscious purpose may even contradict the subconscious purpose.

Because of the continuous inclusion of the interpretation of purpose in the interviews, I de-

16

cided that it was important for me to consider
purpose. The interviewees interpreted purpose on
two levels: the purpose of the initiator of an
item in the ideological training and the purpose
of the item itself. For example: the number of
meetings in a University department, of the Union
of Communist Youth was increased from one to two
a week. The intended purpose of the initiator,
in this case, the department head, is interpreted
as, "to increase the time given to this 'political
- - - -', to make him look good at the Central
Committee". The purpose of the extra meeting itself is interpreted as, "to shove more politics
down our throat".[32] In looking at purpose, I
took a sociological viewpoint: that what is interpreted as purpose can be significant in deter-
mining behavior, and attitude toward behavior.
This is independent of the absolute truth of the
purpose itself. Because of the centralization of
command and control in Romanian society, when
laws, decrees, orders or decisions were passed
down from the top Party or State organ that had
to be implemented in the educational system, sometimes the purpose had been 'lost' on the way down
through the chain of command; or, no purpose, at
least, was given. Whether the intended purpose
was stated or not, students and faculty interpreted purpose, especially on the High School and
University levels. The purpose as interpreted,
then functioned as a distinct stimulus, determin-
ing or modifying behavior.

Section 4: Methods Used in the Field Work

    In gathering information, I used the methods
of observation, participant observation and interview. I was able to observe and be a participant observer in the schools because (a) I was a
lecturer in the University, and (b) because I was
a foreigner.

    Being a lecturer in the University, I had
access to the schools because in Romania, University faculty are generally thought to have special
expertise. As a linguist I was thought to be of

17

use by teachers and administrators as a consultant in the teaching of foreign languages. As a
lecturer I was employed by the State which made
me less a foreigner. I thus escaped some of the
avoidance of foreigners that is officially man-
dated. Generally, I was able to participate in
the normal activity within the educational system.
My observation was not based on pre-arranged
visits to selected classes in selected schools,
so that my research was not that of the visitation
kind.

There were also advantages in being a foreigner. I avoided the normal proving period that
elapses before a Romanian trusts another Romanian.
There were exceptions to this, but this usually
involved a Communist Activist in the educational
institution, such as the Party Secretary. As we
have seen in Part II, Section 2, of this chapter,
as a foreigner I was usually not bound by the
formal strictures of language, so I was able to
ask questions that did not call for stock answers.
Whenever I felt I was getting specially tailored
responses, I cross checked the issue at point with
a larger group of people, either singly or in
group interview.

The interviews were done on a one-to-one basis or with larger numbers. Sometimes interviews
were done in social settings, especially the group
interviews. The social setting gave me access to
people who did not want to be 'seen' alone with a
foreigner outside the school environment. In the
interviewing, the samples were able to be random
only within educational institutions; this applied
especially to the interviewing of students, but
not always to faculty. When the sample could not
be random, I increased the size of the sample. I
had to research those that I could research. As
the research progressed, I concentrated the extended interviews on people whom I had judged in
previous interviews to be well-informed, insight-
ful and forthcoming.

My status as participator increased with my

18

knowledge of the situation. My knowledge of the language also enabled me to participate in normal social situations. But one other factor needs to be mentioned which established my credibility as a participator especially with people whom I was meeting for the first time.

Jokes serve as an important element in the initial or 'phatic communion' stage of Romanian social intercourse.[33] Many of the jokes deal with a character called Bula. Because Bula is a student, the Bula jokes are a favorite of the educational community. Bula is a peasant, over twenty, lacking in brain power, who is still in the fifth grade. My telling a Bula joke or asking for the latest one, frequently served as my introduction when I wanted to interview someone. For some reason, a foreigner telling Bula jokes seemed to appeal to people. Bula jokes often deal with political commentary. Sometimes, in an interview, a Bula joke was used to give me an opinion. Bula jokes are popular with everyone from IVth graders to academicians. In my interviewing, I was often dependent on one faculty member introducing me to another; being able to share Bula jokes would serve as the link, making me acceptable to the new person. Bula pokes fun at the establishment and at educational practices in general. My telling Bula jokes or enjoying other people telling them, signalled that I could look at education satirically. This enhanced my personal credibility and hence, my participatory ability. My telling the Bula jokes also helped me in not being classified as an 'ignorant foreigner'. There are Bula jokes about ignorant foreigners too.

Section 5: Recording the Data

I never used a tape recorder in the observation and interviewing. I tried it in the beginning of the research when interviewing, but permission was always refused. In Romania, there is an acute sensitivity about being recorded, directly or indirectly. I have no evidence about the prevalence of official indirect recordings, but most Romanians think it is prevalent. I sometimes used a tape recorder to record field notes post factum, but always erased the tapes when I had checked them for relevance for my written field notes.

In general I did not take detailed notes during the observations or interviews. During observation I jotted down key words or phrases to serve as headings. I wrote up my field notes after observation and interviews. Some teachers, professors and academicians gave me permission to take notes during interviews. If some entries in my field notes were ambiguous or unclear to me, I rechecked these items. In the case of interviews this was, if possible, with the same person to make sure that the person meant exactly what I had noted in my field notes. If some things were unclear about the observation I rechecked by observation or by informal interview. Many of the interviews were informal, where I started out, for example, with one or two questions and developed the interview on the basis of the replies. This was especially true early on in the research. As the research progressed, my series of questions became more pointed as I sought the answers to specific items.

When interviewing people singly or in groups, I only used my written guide with the faculty whom I interviewed in depth. I never used written questionnaires. I did use oral questionnaires and polls with University students and faculty on the High School and University levels. Interviewing University students in groups of 10-15 made the use of oral questionnaires and polls convenient. Group interview of faculty also facilitated the use of oral questionnaires and polls. In the oral questionnaires and polls, the questions could be answered by a Yes/No reply; at other times the same question was addressed to each individual in the group. An example of the latter type of question was: "What did you do for your patriotic work in September?"

Part III: The Design of the Study

The research was done primarily in the city of Bucharest, the capital of Romania. However, I did visit other educational establishments and interviewed teachers and professors from other municipalities in Romania. In this report I am dealing only with Bucharest because it was only in Bucharest that I did detailed observation. There were two reasons for doing a non-random sampling of the ideological training outside Bucharest. Many Romanians in Bucharest say that outside Bucharest, in the provinces, there is less official pressure and supervision ideologically. I found, and this is not anything more than a quasi-researched impression, that this is not true in the educational system. There are no significant differences in the nature of the ideological training either in content, mode or intensity between the provinces and the nation's capital. This applies only to the municipalities, not to the villages and communes. It also applies only to the educational system and not to other facets of life like agriculture and industry. The only significant differences between the capital and other towns was teachers in the provincial towns stressed that behavior outside of school was minutely known to school officials. This could cause ideological criticism within the school. This could happen in Bucharest also but because of the size of the city, not to the same extent as in the provinces.

Early in the research, because of my own lack of perspicacity, I concentrated on the ideological training as this was administered to the students by teachers and school officials. I realized as my research developed that I could not ignore the ideological training that the teachers continually undergo as well. Reporting exclusively on the training of students by teachers would break the integrated existential situation. The teachers themselves regard the training they are expected to give the students also as training for themselves. This is intended officially.

21

There will be many examples of this in the work
aspect of the training and the organizational aspects, as well as in the more formal and direct
modes of teaching. The continuing training of
the teachers in Party and Union meetings at the
school serves as the immediate source for the
ideological training of the students. It is important then, to also include the continuous
training of the teachers.

To research the genesis of the ideological
training, I chose a Kindergarten, a Grade School,
a High School and a University Department for concentrated study.[34] These four were chosen as focal points. I also chose a number of Kindergartens, Grade Schools, High Schools, and University
Departments as secondary units of research as outlined in Figure 1, where I cross checked what I
found in the focal areas of study. I also interviewed numbers of students, teachers and professors who were not from the focal schools, or the
schools and departments which served as secondary
research units, to check whether the hypotheses
I was looking at were applicable on the broad
scale or if they were confined to one school or a
group of schools. In the report I include only
what is generally applicable. In general, the
schools where I did the focal and secondary research are homogeneous socially. One of the criteria I used in judging relative homogeneity was:
is this a school that parents choose for their
children whom they want, ideally, to go to University?[35] None of the schools was of a kind that
the highest Party Elite use for the education of
their children. However I did interview teachers
from, and University students who had attended,
the Party Elite Schools.[36] There were working
class children in the schools where I did research, but in the schools where I did primary or
secondary research, the proportion of working[37]
class children never exceeded fifty per cent.
I did, however, interview teachers from predomi-
nantly working class schools.[38]

I chose the schools for research which gave

me access to the majority stream in the K-University track. I wanted to look at the genesis and evolution within the educational system, K-University, of the ideological training. Also, this research continuity was possible for me. If I had concentrated on working-class schools, I could have had access to students only to the age of 14. At the age of 14, most students from working-class schools go to trade schools and factory schools, which would have been inaccessible to me. My access to the schools was greatly helped by the Principal of the school hoping I as a University lecturer could be useful as a consultant in the school.

From summary observation and questions about the working-class situation in interviewing, I would suggest that quite different hypotheses would have to be made about the ideological training in the trade schools, for example, than in the purely academic stream, especially with regard to the reception by the students of the training. Briefly, the working-class stream are going to become 'workers' in bloc. The students from the academic stream are vying for limited places in the University, and hence the professional Elite. Ideology is part of the University entrance examination, while there are no ideological requirements for becoming a worker, and no competition. As in many other countries, in Romania, you can become a worker by default. There is no unemployment in Romania, officially, and hence every man can become a worker.

Figure 1 contains the breakdown of the research. The Focal Unit of the research is the institution that served as the central focus of the research. But my research was not the observation and analysis of one institution per se. It was research into a potentially generalizable phenomenon. Hence, corresponding institutions are chosen as Secondary Units of research. The number of interviewees from other corresponding institutions are not included in the first two categories.

23

Type of Educational Institution[a]	Focal Unit	Secondary Units	Students Interviewed			Faculty Interviewed		
			1*	2*	3*	1*	2*	3*
K	1	4	15-20	20-30	10-15	5	12	15
GS	1	6	50-60	30-40	20-30	6	24	90-100
HS	1	5	80-90	120-130	60-70	10	25	340-350
Univ. Dep.	1	2	500-550	70-80	40-50	10	10	90-100+

[a] K= Kindergarten GS= Grade School HS= High School
Univ. Dep.= University Department

* 1= Focal Unit of Research 2= Secondary Unit of Research
3= Other Corresponding Units of Research

+ Includes researchers from Research Institutes,
University Professors and Academicians.

Figure 1: Types & Numbers of Educational Institutions Used in the
Research and Numbers of Faculty and Students Interviewed.

24

Figure 2 shows the average time spent in the
Focal and Secondary Units of research, during the
five academic years, in the period, September
1971 - June 1976. Observation in the early part
of the research served a different purpose than
in the later part. Observation in the second
stage of the research became more refined and
specialized. I would observe to obtain data on
particular hypotheses. For example, in the later
part of my research, one hypothesis I wanted to
test was whether pronouncements from key Party
and State officials given prominence in the media
at a particular time, affected the ideological
training in the schools, at the same time or
shortly thereafter.

Figure 3 shows the ratio, expressed in percentage, of students who were interviewed in individual or small group interviews, two to three
in the group, and the percentage of students who
were interviewed in larger groups of over three.
Because the majority of students were interviewed
in larger groups, there is no breakdown into
Focal, Secondary, and General Units as there is
with Faculty in Figure 4. The interviews took
place in the educational institutions or in informal settings, at parties, at birthdays, on out-
ings, on social occasions in general. The last
also gave me an opportunity to interview parents.
However, parent reaction to children's ideological training in the school is not included in this
report. I will refer to these interviews in the
conclusion when I refer to the development of
potential hypotheses about the efficacy of the
ideological training in Romania.

The numbers of university students interviewed is very high in proportion to the numbers of
kindergarten children, both in gross numbers and
in numbers interviewed singly. There are three
reasons for this. As a university lecturer, access to university students was comparatively easy
for me. Secondly, I was interested in the evolution of the ideological training, K-University. I
used interviews with University students to learn

25

Educational Institution		Focal Unit	Secondary Unit
YEAR 1	K	2	2
	GS	2	2
	HS	2	2
	Univ.	8	2
Yearly Total:		490	245
YEAR 2	K	1	1
	GS	3	2
	HS	3	2
	Univ.	10	3
Yearly Total:		595	280
YEAR 3	K	1	0
	GS	2	2
	HS	2	1
	Univ.	10	1
Yearly Total:		525	140
YEAR 4	K	1	1
	GS	1	1
	HS	1	1
	Univ.	4	1
Yearly Total:		245	140
YEAR 5	K	1/2	1
	GS	2	3
	HS	4	1
	Univ.	5	2
Yearly Total:		402	245

Figure 2: Average Hours Spent in Focal And Secondary Units Per Week during Research Period.

Type of Educational Institution	Students Interviewed	
	Individual or Small Group	Larger Group
K	10%	90%
GS	15%	85%
HS	20%	80%
Univ. Dep.	40%	60%

Figure 3: Ratio of Individual/Small Group And Larger Group Interviewing of Students.

Type of Educational Institution	Focal	Secondary	General
K	100%[a]	60%[a]/40%[b]	20%[a]/80%[b]
GS	100%[a]	30%[a]/70%[b]	15%[a]/85%[b]
HS	100%[a]	75%[a]/25%[b]	8%[a]/92%[b]
Univ. Dep.	100%[a]	100%[a]	20%[a]/80%[b]

[a]Individual or Small Group Interview

[b]Larger Group Interview

Figure 4: Ratio of Individual/Small Group and Larger Group Interviewing of Faculty in the Various Units of Research.

about their training in the lower schools.
Thirdly, I concentrated on University students because they are the future Elite of the country,
both on the political level and the intellectual/
professional level. Political scientists in
dealing with communist nations have concentrated
very largely on the Elite element. Bertrand
Russell, six years after the Russian revolution,
stated that Marxism, because of its Hegelian base,
would produce an elite society for the good of
"vigorous administrators having a good position in
the official hierarchy, and probably to no one
else".[39]   Hugh Setson-Watson in The Eastern European Revolution, stressed the importance of the
role of the intellectuals and their consequent
consolidation in a communist revolution.[40]   Because of the importance of university education as
the sine qua non rite for passage into the Elite,
on the State and Party level, I am hoping that my
treatment of ideological training on the university level, will be a contribution to communist
studies in general. The contribution will however be a political sociology, not political
science, which in general considers only the existence or non-existence of a university education
in a particular person, without considering what
happens to the university student in his or her
ideological training.

Because the majority of students and some
faculty were interviewed in larger groups I put
the figures in approximate numbers to cater for
the times when some people were not present for
all the sessions. Sometimes the numbers of interviewees in the general category is far greater
than those in the focal unit, as for example with
High School Faculty. But in Figure 4 it can be
seen that the faculty in the focal unit were interviewed on a one-to-one basis while 92% of the
general group were interviewed in groups of more
than three. Also, many of the faculty were interviewed on many different occasions so that the interviews were extensive, both longitudinally and
in depth. More than 50% of the faculty in all of
the focal units were interviewed over the whole

period of the research. More than 20% of the
faculty in the secondary units were interviewed
over the five years also. The interviews of individual faculty in the focal and secondary units
amounted to 20-60 hours of individual interviewing time over the five year period.

Part IV: Validity of the Study

Howard S. Becker in his volume of collected
essays, Sociological Work, addresses the question
of validity in sociological studies using field
work from the point of view of the method and design used in both the study itself and the documentation of the method and design in the reporting of the study. In the third chapter of the
same volume, Field Work Evidence, Becker introduces the notion of credibility as an extension of
the notion of validity. The chapter begins with
the question: "How credible are the conclusions
derived from data gathered by field work?"[41]
Credibility for Becker deals not only with the
truth or non-truth of the content of the reported
material; credibility depends on the method and
design of the study that has been reported using
methods that are acceptable scientifically. In
another work, Boys in White, a classic in the reporting of field work methods, Becker stresses the
aspect of replication.[42] My study in the main can
be replicated. On the basis of the report, hypotheses can be developed about ideological training in general, leading to a general theory about
the use of the educational system, for example, as
the instrument in teaching values that are not
generated or reinforced by the culture.

My role in the research was that of collator
and organizer. Only the conceptualization that
organizes the facts is mine. There is no use of
esoteric models that were preconceived as hypotheses and imposed on the ideological training in
situ. My study is the collating and organizing of
common sense.[43] In Romania, there is a keen consciousness of the ideological training. What I
report belongs very closely to the Romanian common

sense.

It is important to understand this point in the Romanian context specifically, because in Romania the source of the ideological training comes from the apex of the centralized power. In Romania, a distinct consciousness persists that the aspects in the ideological training regarded as communist are being 'done to them', at all levels in the educational system which is in itself a centrally structured system. The initiation of the ideological training is a force outside the control of the teachers and professors. The centralization of the power of initiating ideology is not only admitted by the highest organs of the Communist Party and Government in Romania, but constitutes an important part of the ideological training itself, on the theoretical and practical level.

There is then, in Romania, a heightened consciousness about the communist aspects of the ideological training itself. I was not studying something like peer influence in the socialization process, which may be largely sub-conscious and automatic, and therefore difficult to research. I was studying an overt ideology 'given from on high', which the people should follow. I am not reporting on whether this ideology is accepted as belief. I am simply reporting an overt, observable phenomenon. That the ideological training is still a very conscious phenomenon, is shown by the fact that the leaders of the country time and time again say that the presently accpeted values are not politically acceptable. The people must adopt with enthusiasm the new values of the new socialist society.[44]

Modifying a model that political scientists use in comparative politics,[45] we can say that Romania now is in a state of mobilization politically. It does not seek a consensus and all participation must follow the lines of the mobilization. The participation is not a question of choice. There is no opting out, or unofficial discussion

of the mobilization. Because of this mobilization then, there is a consciousness by teachers
and students of the ideological training that one
would not expect to find, for example, of the socialization process in an American Public School
where usually the teachers are not mobilized to
teach values which are not part of their own culture.[46] Using the mobilization/participation model in talking about Romania does not imply a value
judgment with regard to Communism or the system in
Romania. My modification of the model is one used
by the President of Romania, Nicolae Ceausescu,[47]
who wants only a participation which mirrors the
mobilization. Active participation in society is
exclusive to the model presented in mobilization.
But Ceausescu does not want a state coerced. He
wants a state that adopts the ideological training
that is now proposed in the schools, so that one
people will be united in one ideological unit.
The proposal and content of the ideological training is mobilization; the content of the training
is not arrived at by consensus. In turn, the Romanians are conscious of this training because
they are being asked to change not only their observable behavior, but also their attitudes, their
thoughts, their values. People must not only participate in the mobilization, but participate en-
thusiastically.

In Romania the training is overt, direct, and
highly observable. I am not then, reporting a
socialization process that is indirect or subconscious, which has a multiple source. So the validity of reporting the observed does not pose a
major problem in itself, because of the nature of
the observed and the consequent potential replication of the study.

The problems in my research come not from the
material studied but from the difficulty in gaining access to the material studied, especially for
a foreigner. To research is to be critical. In
Romania the source of truth is regarded in an essentially Marxist-Leninist way. Truth derives
from official policy and currently accepted ideol-

ogy. The truth-value of a proposition depends on its conformity to a currently acceptable or accepted notion. The policy and the ideology may change, as we will see for example, in Chapter III, but the ontological and epistemological parameter which determines the nature and knowledge of reality and prepositions about reality remains the same.

In Romania, the social sciences are essentially deductive sciences. In the section dealing with the period since 1946, in a history of Romania published in 1970, we are told that the social sciences "went through an extraordinary advancement after the liberation of the country by using the classic works of Marx, Engels, Lenin and the literature of our Party" (the Romanian Communist Party).[48] In Romania if there is assessment, then it is only official assessment, to isolate what is weak and needing remedy. Policy in general, which would include the ideological training in the schools, is something that is carried out, not something that is examined. I am not sure whether it is feasible to talk about absolute neutrality in research in the areas of the social sciences anywhere in the world, but Romania officially takes a biblical attitude: you are for or against the official doctrine, hot or cold, because all research should be evaluation done from an official viewpoint or framework with the intention of improving the training. Foreigners, unless they are professed communists and card-carrying members of the Communist Party, are automatically presumed to be against the official policy, and so are normally barred from the opportunity to observe unless in so far as possible, in controlled situations. Even foreign communists are usually highly controlled.

The difficulties in the replication of the study, then comes not from anything inherent in the nature of the material studied, but from extrinsic factors belonging to the realm of social control and censorship on the governmental level.

NOTES

1. Gabriel A. Almond and G. Bingham Powell, Jr.,
   <u>Comparative Politics: a developmental ap-
   proach</u>. Boston and Toronto: Little, Brown
   and Co., 1966.

   Harold J. Laski, <u>A Grammar of Politics</u>. London:
   George Allen and Unwin, 1934.

   Bertrand de Jouvenel, <u>Sovereignty</u>. trans., J.
   F. Huntington, Chicago: University of Chicago
   Press, 1953.

2. Margaret Mead, "National Character," in <u>Anthro-
   pology Today</u>, by A. L. Kroeber, ed., Chicago:
   University of Chicago Press, 1953.

   Eric Fromm, <u>The Nature of Man</u>. New York:
   Macmillan, 1969.

   John J. Honigmann, <u>Culture and Personality</u>.
   New York: Harper, 1954.

3. This is the same assumption operative in the
   'Melting Pot'-school of history of education
   in the U.S. See: Colin Greer, <u>The Great
   School Legend</u> (New York: Penguin Books, 1976),
   pp. 33-58.

4. Anthony F. C. Wallace, <u>Culture and Personality</u>
   (New York: Random House, 1970), p. 25.

5. <u>Six Keys to the Soviet System</u> (Boston: The
   Beacon Press, 1956), p. 53.

6. Wallace, op. cit., p. 22.

7. <u>Ibid</u>., p. 23.

8. See: Nicolae Ceausescu, Report at the National
   Conference of the Romanian Communist Party
   (Bucharest: Meridiane Publishing House, 1972),
   pp. 11-12.

9. Ivan Volgyes, "East European Socialization", Problems of Communism, (Jan.-Feb., 1974), pp. 46-56.

10. (New York: Praeger, 1975), p. 98.

11. Kurt Kwasny, "Ungarns Kommunisten Wagen Mehr Democratie", Osteuropa, (November, 1971), pp. 842-850. Referred to in: Ibid., p. 138.

12. Field Notes, December, 1975. The Professor is also a member of the Academy.

13. Field Notes, January, 1972. High School, Focal Unit of research.

14. I am making an operational distinction between Marxist and Marxian. Marxist is something directly from Marx; Marxian is something that comes indirectly from Marx or the Marxist tradition.

15. Trond, op. cit., pp. 87-8.

16. Ion Ratiu, Contemporary Romania (Richmond, England: Foreign Affairs Publishing Co., Ltd., 1975), p. 64. For a summary of this 'mini-revolution' see: Trond, op. cit., pp. 62-8.

17. The frequent use of this model started in the thirties, with numerous works appearing after World War II using the model of totalitarianism to compare fascist Germany and Italy with the communist countries in Eastern Europe. For the more famous of these works, see: Karl Popper, The Open Society and its Enemies. London: Kegan Paul, 1945.

    Hannah Arendt, The Origins of Totalitarianism. New York: Harcourt, Brace, 1957.

    Carl J. Friedrich & Zbigniew K. Brzezinski, Totalitarian Dictatorship and Autocracy. Cambridge, Mass.: Harvard University Press, 1956.

18. Ghita Ionescu in his brief but monumental survey of Comparative Communist Politics (London: Macmillan, 1972), devotes the whole book to a discussion of the problem of the lack of a commonly accepted method in comparative communist politics.

19. Chicago: University of Chicago Press, 1960.

20. Ibid., p. v.

21. Ibid., p. 2.

22. In the volume of collected essays: Howard S. Becker, Sociological Work (New Brunswick, N. J.: Transaction Books, 1977), p. 121.

23. See: C. Ionescu-Bujor, Higher Education in Romania. Bucharest: Meridiane Publishing House, 1964.

    A. Manolache, General Education in Romania. Bucharest: Meridiane Publishing House, 1965.

    Dumitru Muster & Gheorghe Vaideanu, "Romania: Contemporary Romanian Education", Journal of Education, Vol. 152 (February, 1970), pp. 64-71.

24. By 'visitation' literature I mean literature that shows little evidence of scholarship or expertise in the sociocultural aspects of the society where the education is studied. Many studies on Soviet & Chinese education fall into this category where the time spent in the country was short, if any, and there is no evidence of knowledge of the language, or languages spoken in the country.

25. Columbus, Ohio: Charles E. Merrill Publishing Co., 1969.

26. The State's Secrets Act of 12/24/1971, has strict regulations about communication with foreigners. See: Ratiu, op. cit., p. 67.

From the interviews I learned that every
meeting with a foreigner must be reported in
detail to the police, even a casual meeting
on the street, as in the case of a foreigner
asking for directions. I did not interview
for this kind of information but I was told
because I was a foreigner and the interviewee
was a Romanian talking to me. People do not
report every meeting, but failure to report
can cause a visit from the Security police.

27. This question raises important anthropolin-
    guistic problems dealing with the public ex-
    pression of sentiment as it is coded in dif-
    ferent languages. The following are two ex-
    amples of the code in Romanian for the ex-
    pression of patriotic sentiment; both are
    taken from a Grade IV and Grade V class and
    the translation is literal: "Oh! my country,
    with beautiful eyes", and "Romania, my heart,
    my soul, my love, sweet and beautiful". The
    linguistic principle in the theory of trans-
    lation, of translating codes not words is of
    little use in these instances; but the ob-
    server would miss important material if these
    utterances were not translated, or if given
    non-literal translations.

28. For example, denigrating the good name of Ro-
    mania is punishable by loss of citizenship.
    See: Ibid.

29. This raises a complex linguistic problem. The-
    oretical ideological training in Romania is
    given primarily in 'formal Romanian' (Limba
    literara, lit., 'literary Romanian'); atti-
    tude is usually expressed in colloquial lan-
    guage. If one wants personal rather than
    publicly acceptable answers, it is important
    to use an informal code in the interviewing.
    Using the formal code in discussing ideologi-
    cal training is usually equated with a non-
    trust role relationship.

30. For example: if a male says in greeting to a

36

female <u>Sarut</u> <u>mina</u> (lit., 'I kiss the hand'),
this can signify a political attitude as well
as a greeting. The expression is officially
discouraged, as is the hand-kissing practice
that sometimes accompanies it, as a relic of
the bourgeoisie. The respective use or non-
use of the expression by a Party Secretary or
Dean is a useful signal as code, indicating
Political role and attitude. If the expression is given the dictionary translation
(Dictionar Roman Englez, Ed. a 111-a. Bucharest: Editura Stintifica, 1973), 'my respects/
compliments to you', the role significance of
the expression is neutralized.

31. Field Notes, May, 1975. The 'this' and 'that'
    refer to ideological items.

32. Field Notes, April, 1973. Interview with stu-
    dent in University, Focal Unit of research.
    The student was an official in the Union of
    Communist Youth.

33. This is the Malinowski notion that each cul-
    ture has ritual formulae used in social dis-
    course that serve as the introductory phase
    for two people, or when there is nothing to
    communicate. In England, for example there
    can be discussion about the weather, in Ro-
    mania, jokes. See: B. Malinowski, "The Prob-
    lem of meaning in primitive languages", in C.
    K. Ogden and I. A. Richards, <u>The Meaning of</u>
    <u>Meaning</u>. London: Routledge & Kegan Paul,
    1923.

34. In Romanian these are: <u>Gradinita</u>, <u>Scoala</u>
    <u>Generala</u>, <u>Liceu</u> and <u>Facultate</u>. I am not
    naming the schools for the sake of anonymity;
    I am keeping structural information to a mini-
    mum for the same reason.

35. In Romania, as generally in Europe, entry into
    University is the normal rite for passage in-
    to the middle-class or the elite. In Romania,
    some schools, starting with Kindergarten, are

regarded as University track schools.

36. By Party Elite Schools I mean schools chosen
for their children by the highest Communist
Party and State officials: the extended family of the President and the Prime Minister
and in general the children of members of the
Permanent Praesidium, the Central Committee,
the Executive Committee. On the state side,
children of the Council of Ministers for example and of the Trade Unions Central Council
attend these Elite schools.

37. I found out this information by asking a random sample of home-room teachers in the particular school. In Romania, parental occupation of students is well known to peers and
teachers. Questions about parental occupation
and income do not belong in general to the
'intimate' category in Romania.

38. Working class schools are generally in Bucharest, the grade schools in certain suburbs
and trade schools in general. Children of
the intellectual Elite who live near predomi-
nantly working class schools often travel into the city to university track grade schools.

39. Bertrand Russell, "Freedom in Education: A
Protest against Mechanism", Dial, LXXIV,
(Feb., 1923), p. 160.

40. Hugh Setşon-Watson, The East European Revolution. London: Methuen, 1950. Setson-Watson
seems to use the term intellectual as it is
used today in Romania, as denoting someone
who is a university graduate.

41. op. cit., p. 39.

42. Howard S. Becker et al. (Chicago: University
of Chicago Press, 1961), p. 30.

43. See: Jack D. Douglas (ed.), Understanding
Everyday Life. London: Routledge & Kegan

Paul, 1971.

Jack D. Doublas et al., Existential Sociology.
Cambridge & New York: Cambridge University
Press, 1977.

44. See: Scinteia November 3-9, 1971 for articles
and the reporting of speeches of prominent
figures in the Communist Party that lament
the continual adherence to the 'old' bourgeois
values, and the lack of enthusiasm in the
adoption of, and devotion to the new Socialist values. There are many entrances in my
field notes where students, teachers, and
professors reported being lectured for their
individual or group failure in adopting the
new values of Socialism and Communism, their
lack of enthusiasm in promoting these values
actively, and for their lip-service to the
Party and its system of governance.

45. Ghita Ionescu, op. cit., p. 55.

46. A possible exception to this in the U.S., will
be the new policy of multi-cultural education,
if it is adopted as a program in the schools.
See: Frank H. Klassen & Donna M. Gollnick,
Pluralism and the American Teacher. AACTE,
1977.

47. Trond, op. cit., pp. 97-8.

48. Miron Constantinescu et al. Istoria Romaniei.
(Bucuresti: Editura Didactica si Pedagogica,
1970), p. 608.

CHAPTER II

ROMANIA: THE POLITICAL AND STATE STRUCTURES

Romania only became a nation in the latter half of the 19th century. It is still a country where political consciousness, of both internal and external political status, is an important part of the individual and social psychological make-up. The very spelling of the name of the country involves a political stand; the contemporary spelling, Romania, stresses the Latinity of the ancestry of the country's population which is surrounded on all sides by Slavs and Magyars.[1] For a period after 1944, the official spelling was the more Slavic Rominia.

In Part I of the introduction I want to consider briefly, certain salient aspects of Romania's geography, political structure and economy, especially the factors which concern education and the ideological training in the school system. In Part II of the Introduction, I will consider the educational system in general in Romania.

Part I: Geography, Political Structure and Economy
Section 1: Geography

In The Geography of Romania, by Academician Tiberiu Morariu et al., we read:

As a result of the new situation established after World War II, today Romania has friendly countries on all its borders: the USSR to the east and north, the People's Republic of Bulgaria to the south, the Federal Socialist Republic of Yugoslavia to the south-west, and the Hungarian People's Republic to the west.[2]

Romania also has the Black Sea as part of its eastern frontier. Before World War II, Romania also had borders with Poland and Czechoslovakia, making it the eighth largest country in Europe.[3] Romania "covers an area of nearly 92,000 square miles, which is almost the same as the area of the United Kingdom. It is rather larger than the state of Minnesota, but smaller than Colorado".[4] Romania's 800 miles of frontier with the USSR is its longest border line.[5]

The Socialist Republic of Romania, not only belongs to the group of countries that are commonly referred to as Eastern Europe, where the Communist Party rules in each of the group, but it has no borders with a non-Communist country.[6] The latter was brought to my attention in many of the interviews I had with students and educators, and also with writers and artists in general. A contemporary Romanian poet explained Romania's geography like this:

We do not blame the West for sacrificing us after the war. Our geography is our fate. We are the lamb of Europe, neither in central Europe or the Balkans. If Hungary and Yugoslavia and Czechoslovakia were to be communist, then we had to be communist too. Politically and aesthetically, they could not afford to destroy the red vista with the Romanian white capitalist that was also non-Slavic. Marx was right. There is a determinism, an evolution that is blind. But for us Romanians, this determinism is geographical, not historical. Place is more important than time.[7]

When I started my research in Romania in 1971, the population of Romania was 20,400,000, which ranks Romania with the countries of comparative density in the world.[8] The percentage of workers in 1970 was given as 76% of the total population.[9] In Romania people are classified officially in three categories: workers, peasants and intellectuals. There is a problem in fixing the exact numbers of non-ethnic Romanians who live in Romania because the census allows non-ethnic Romanians to be classified as Romanians, if they say their primary language is Romanian. The census on March 15, 1966 had put the percentage of ethnic

Romanians at 87.7%, ethnic Hungarians at 8.5%,
ethnic Germans, including both Saxons and Schwabians, at 2.0%, with Gypsies, Ukranians (including
Ruthenians and Hutans), Serbs, Croats, Slovenes,
Russians, Jews, Tartars, Slovaks and other groups
making up the rest.[10] But it is important to note
that some minorities in Romania, notably the Hungarians, Germans, and Jews, are significantly
more urbanized than the ethnic Romanians. Many of
the Hungarians and the Germans live in concentrated areas making their presence in those particular
areas either dominant or significant.[11] As we
shall see later, the issue of minorities becomes
an item in the ideological training in Romania in
the schools even though research on the question
of minorities is officially taboo.[12]

Section 2: The Communist Party

     In Romania "The Romanian Communist Party is
the leading force of the whole of society".[13] It
is difficult to talk sensibly about the social
composition of the Communist Party because officially in Romania there cannot exist social classes. Gilberg Trond, using a variety of official
and non-official sources, put the numbers of Party
members in 1972 at 2,281,372, stating that, "Pro-
portionately the RCP is one of the largest Communist parties in the world".[14] If the Trond figures
for social composition are accepted, in 1972, of
these members of the RCP, 46.5% were workers, 23.1%
were peasants and 18.8% were intellectuals. These
last statistics however do not reveal the dominance of the intellectuals in entering into the
ruling echelon of the Party, or the proportionate
number of the intelligentsia, as a group, in the
Party.

     In the educational institutions where I did
research, in both the Focal units and Secondary
units of research, more than 80% of the Grade
School teachers were members of the Party, 84% of
the High School teachers were members and 92% of
the University faculty were. An official of the
Writers' Union of Bucharest said in an interview

in May 1974, that more than 90% of the writers in
Bucharest were members of the Party; the figures
for some other groups of intelligentsia in Bucharest also were over 90%.[15] Mobility within a
profession or an institution, as well as other
benefits like foreign travel, is difficult for
non-members of the Party. Social mobility within
an institution and benefits like foreign travel
are phenomena found more among the intelligentsia
than the workers who have little opportunity for
institutional mobility. Party membership consequently is more important for the intelligentsia
than for workers, because of the potential advantages for the intelligentsia.

    In the period, 1971-1976, when I did research
in Romania, there were drives to increase the numbers of workers and peasants in the Party. In
political representation in general, women and
youth were also given special attention.[16] Of 100
University students surveyed in 1974-'75, 100%
said that they would join the Party or had already
joined it.[17] The constant reason given, was future protection and advantage. Job security and
advantage would be impossible without Party membership, because even on a negative plane, non-
membership is the criterion used to guage lack of
support for the system, lack of enthusiasm, even
opposition. Even the 1965 Constitution states
that citizens who are progressive and conscientious become members of the Party. On a positive
level, many jobs require Party membership.

    Membership of the Party involves regular at-
tendance at Party meetings, usually weekly, in
one's designated group or cell. This is normally
at one's place of work. For example, teachers
would be members of the school cell, university
faculty of the department cell. Each cell is subject to a cell on a higher level. Above the cell,
there is the district level, then the county level
and national level. But there is always a connec-
tion between each level, by the inclusion in a
higher cell of members that belong to the cells in
the group directly below. No cell operates on its

44

own, but always on orders and program brought back
by the member, usually the Party Secretary, who
belongs to the higher cell.[18]

On the national level of the Communist Party
there is the National Party Conference or Congress, which is an elected body and represents the
district level and county level cells. This meets
every four years normally. When it is not in
session, the organs of the National Congress are
the power centers of the Party nationally.

Political scientists who are interested in
communist studies frequently concentrate on the
composite membership of the national organs because these organs are regarded as the key centers
of power in communist nations. The Standing
Praesidium in Romania, formerly called the Political Bureau, and corresponding for example, to the
Politbureau in the USSR, is the highest Party organ. The other important organs are the Secretariat and the Executive Committee. Organizationally,
these three organs are part of the Central Committee which can also meet as a Plenum to issue important decrees which have the force of law. It
is from these organs that some of the ideological
training in the school originates. For example,
we read in the report of the National Conference
of the Romanian Communist Party, July 19-21, 1972,
given by Nicolae Ceausescu, the President of Romania and member of all of the above Party organs:
"the Plenary Meeting of the Central Committee of
November 3-5 (1971), approved a vast programme of
improving and amplifying the ideological and socialist educational activity".[19]

These national organs of the Party also periodically inspect the ideological state of and
training in, an educational institution. These
Party inspectors are usually alternate members of
the Executive Committee of the RCP.[20]

During the research period, 1971-'76, the
President of Romania, Nicolae Ceausescu, as the
General Secretary of the Party and its chief ideo-

logue, was the driving force behind the ideology of Romania.[21] Many books and articles refer to Romania as 'Ceausescu's Romania'. Much of the literature, both official and non-official, contains detailed treatment of the importance of Ceausescu in the understanding of Romania today. This can range from praise in both official and non-official literature,[22] to criticism in the non-official literature, accusing Ceausescu of the crimes of 'personality cult' and dictatorship.[23] He becomes an important part of the ideological training in the schools, both for his words and actions, but also for his status as a personality.

> The frequent ideological campaigns in Romania are therefore more than mere Party manipulations designed to concentrate control in one apparat in opposition to other emerging elites; the campaigns represent the carrying out of a strong moral conviction of the part of the undisputed Party leader. It follows from his conviction that Ceausescu is not content to play the part of merely political leader. His program is moral and ethical as well, and the general secretary is constantly involved in discussion with, and exhortations to, educators, writers, artists, and playwrights to ensure that his wideranging views are clear to all citizens and moral-cultural elites. Ceausescu has become a self-appointed authority in fields that nowadays are generally left to others, even in socialist states.[24]

A: The Union of Communist Youth

The 'reserve' of the Romanian Communist Party is the Union of Communist Youth (UCY).[25] Membership of the UCY includes young workers and soldiers, but it is also the organization to which High School and University students belong, where they receive part of their ideological training in school. The UCY becomes an integral part of the school curriculum, but it can also flow into activities outside the school. Membership of the Central Committee of the UCY is regarded as an important step in an important Party, and/or State career. The Secretary General of the UCY is usually a member of one of the important organs of the Romanian Communist Party, and is usually not a youth.[26]

The UCY also incorporates the Union of Students' Associations of Romania (USAR) which is specifically for students in tertiary education, which in'turn has a sub-branch for University Students, The Union of Communist Students.

Part of the ideological training in the school system of Romania will come through membership in these organizations. The High School student will be a member of the UCY. The University student will be a member of the UCY, the Union of University Students and maybe of the Communist Party as well, each with its own separate weekly meetings and activities. Student officers of these organizations sit on faculty councils in schools and Universities as well as on the University Senate. In turn, faculty participate as official consultants and guides in the organizations.

Section 3: The State Structure

We have been dealing up to now with the Communist Party structure in Romania and its involvement with ideological training. In Romania the CP is also the principal factor on the State level.

The State organization in Romania is organized on the district level which may be a commune or a sector within a municipality. Above the district and municipality, there is the County level (judet).[27] Starting with the district and including the County, there is a People's Council, an elected body. But it is the Communist Party that controls the elections and candidates for election to the People's Council and only Party members can sit on the Executive Committees of the People's Councils.[28] For the appointment of Kindergarten

47

administrators it is the Executive Committee of
the People's Council on the County level that
makes the recommendation for appointment. The
grade school administrator is appointed by the
School Inspectorate of the local district People's
Council, but the School Inspectorate is directly
subject to the Executive Committee of the People's
Council for Education and Culture. The administration for General High Schools, where I did the
High School research, is appointed by the School
Inspectorate on the County level of the People's
Council. This inspectorate is also subject to
the Executive Committee of the People's Council
on the County level. Hence, all administration
positions in schools are under the direct control
of the Communist Party's nomenclatura or power of
appointment.

On the State level, nationally, the State
Council and the Grand National Assembly have
legislative functions, and may, for example, enact laws including laws governing education. But
in general, the initiative in governance comes
from the Council of Ministers which is the body
that controls the country exclusively. The Ministry of Education comes under the Council of Ministers with its own Minister of Education. The Ministry of Education runs the schools of the country,
deciding policy, text-books, budget, and standards
in a centralized way. The Executive Committees on
the district and County level, for the most part,
implement the decisions of the Ministry of Education, which is located in the capital, Bucharest.
The Assistant Minister of Education is also the
Chairman of the National Council of Pioneer Organizations.[29]   The Pioneers, which is the Communist
organization for the K-Grade School group, is usually in other communist countries in the Party organization not, as in Romania, on the State level.
It was moved to the State level in 1966 because,
to quote Nicolae Ceausescu's words from the meeting
when the change was announced: "Young children of
Pioneer age need a lot of guidance from experienced teachers who have a well-developed scientific
training behind them and an understanding of the

48

children spiritually."[30] In the report on the research, we shall explore the implications of
teachers being responsible for the Pioneer activities of the students rather than Party activists.

The importance of the Party control over the
State is summed up by Gilberg Trond as follows:

The power of the Party in ideological matters
and its control over the top decision-making
positions in the governmental apparats, planning agencies, and academia allow the top
political leadership close control over lower levels of the elite structures as well.
Individuals can be quickly rerouted, dis-
missed or promoted in accordance with the
Party's wishes. Reorganization and trans-
fers can be accomplished relatively rapidly
if not smoothly. The RCP is in charge of the
'nomenclatura' of all major societal elites,
a fact that is of the utmost importance in
ensuring decision making in correspondence [31]
with the Party program.

Section 4: The Economy

Economically, Romania belongs to the ranks
of developing countries. It is a country that is
pressing ahead with industrialization and a rate
of reinvestment that makes Romania one of the
leaders in the world in reinvested income. In-
vestment in the 1976-1980 Five Year Plan is to be
equal to the whole period of 1960-1975, a period [32]
of three Five Year Plans. John M. Montias in
his important work on Romanian development starts
his work with a summary statement:

Industrial output has indeed grown very fast;
health conditions have vastly improved; education has spread; new technical skills have
been developed; and consumption levels have
risen since the late 1930's not only because
the majority of peasants and industrial workers live somewhat better but also because so
many peasant families have moved to town and

49

acceeded to the higher standards of urban
living.[33]

In his Modernization in Romania since World
War II,[34] Gilberg Trond points out that modernization in Romania has primarily been concentrated
on industrialization which, in 1930, absorbed only 7.9% of the population, and was confined to a
few areas dealing mostly with light and consumer
goods industries, even though Romania is the
richest of all countries in Eastern Europe in
minerals and fuels. While total investments in
the Romanian economy have risen 20 times between
1938-1971, material production and especially industry, has taken 80% of all funds invested. Of
the remaining 20%, social-cultural investments
which include education have taken a much higher
percentage increase than services.[35]

In 1971, agriculture, which since the advent
of communism has received little increase in in-
vestment, received only 16.7% of total investments
while being "still Romania's leading single activity", occupying 47% of the total work force in
1972, with a contribution to the national income
of only 24.8%.[36] The attention agriculture gets
in Romania is seasonal, at planting and harvesting
time which also involves student participation and
ideological training, on both a theoretical and
practical level.

Because the concerted drive towards industrialization and the emphasis on productive personnel
results in low salaries for non-productive personnel, among whom are included students, teachers,
and professors, the economic situation also has an
effect on the ideological training. The same policy which results in little attention to services,
transport, and consumer goods in general, also has
an important influence on reaction to the ideological training in the schools.

. . . the industrial expansion has been so
rapid, that it has strained the whole socio-
economic system to the utmost. The trans-

50

portation and service sectors have not been
able to keep up with the output facilities,
causing massive bottlenecks and waste. The
social sector is underdeveloped and has not
been able to provide adequate facilities in
such areas as housing and sanitation for the
growing urban population.[37]

Industrialization is an important stage in
the Marxist continuum and was also stressed by
Lenin. Stalin implemented the theory of the ideo-
logues and developed a process of industrialization for the Soviet Union which was also adopted
for Romania after the War. But it was Romania's
plan to industrialize in a way that was not in
conformity with the Soviet Union, and Comecon, the
economic organization of the so-called Iron Curtain bloc countries, that has influenced much of
the ideological training in the schools today, especially with regard to nationalism and patriotism,
but also with regard to relations between nations
of all political persuasion.

At the end of 1961, Comecon as a group and
the Soviet Union in particular, opposed the com-
plete industrialization of another communist bloc
country, in this case Romania. This is a significant period for much of the subsequent ideological
training in the schools in Romania. Romania started to turn to herself as the determiner of her own
role and destiny, but always within a framework
however that would not lead to a Budapest '56 or a
Prague '68. Romania started to seek her own relations with the world outside Comecon, both economically and politically. Many older teachers and
professors mention that this was the period when
there was the beginning of a new era in the ideological training in the schools.

Czechoslovakia and East Germany wanted Romania to be a supplier of raw materials for their
industrially advanced economy. Poland, Hungary,
and even Bulgaria, which was in the same position
as Romania industrially, criticized Romania for
acting alone outside the general socialist-bloc

plan, which had been drawn up to avoid duplication in order to make the bloc a meaningful unity, not only politically, but also economically. Romania regarded the plan as economic imperialism directed against a developing country, in this case herself. Romania turned to nationalism in the ideological training and adopted a position about international relations and national development which is still part of the ideological training in the schools. The early '60's is also the beginning of Romania's virtual withdrawal from the socialist-bloc military alliance, the Warsaw Pact.[38]

Part II: The Structure of the Romanian Educational System
Section 1: The Evolution of Education since the advent of Communism in Romania

With the advent of communism in Romania after World War II, there also began a reform of the educational system using the Soviet system as a model. This reform took final form in August of 1948. All the educational institutions were nationalized. This is still the case except for the institutions for the training of the clergy for the Romanian Orthodox Church. Schools were to be used for the propagation of Marxist-Leninist principles; their organization was also to be modelled on these same principles.[39] Romania also made the eradication of illiteracy one of its goals, which it achieved in a comparatively short period.[40]

The reform of education which took place in the middle '50's was not as extreme as in 1948. The primary and secondary streams were made a continuous unit. The continuity was necessary because of the steadily advancing national standard of education in the country and the gradual improvement in the economy. Higher education was to become more geared to training students for a modern economy which resulted in the improvement in polytechnical education. But special attention was also being paid to the ideological training of the students. Stalin was dead. The Communist

Party in Romania had achieved greater stability
with the disappearance of the fear of internal opposition to the communist regime. The jockeying[41]
for power within the Party had abated. The cult
of Stalinism and the Stalinist position on the
role of the Soviet Union as the true fatherland of
all Romanians had to be replaced. Rule by terror
in Romania was not as intense as it had been in
the '46-'54 period. The section of the RCP which
deals with propaganda was becoming more sophisti-
cated with the new blood joining the section; the[42]
new members were university educated personnel.

As we have seen already in Part I, Romania
began to become less dependent on the Soviet Union
and the Organizations of the Communist Eastern
European countries in the '60's. There was in
general a de-Russification in Romanian society
which also was reflected in the educational sys-[43]
tem. This culminated in the reforms of 1968
which brought about, in the main, the structure of
the system of education in Romania which was still[44]
in force in 1971-1976, the period of my research.
There was also appointed in 1969 a new Minister of
Education, Miron Constantinescu, a man who had
held prominent position in the Party until his
purge in 1957. He belonged to a family who had
been instrumental in founding the Socialist Party
in Romania. He himself had been reared in a mid-
dle-class family. He was a highly educated man
who also had been a communist 'illegalist' during
the war period; he spent most of the war years in
prison where his wife, also a political prisoner,
died in 1942. He had held high offices on the
Party and State levels until the mid-'50's, but
had been purged in 1957 because of his reputation
as a cultural liberalizer and his popularity among
the intellectuals. His bourgeois background, his
intellectual stature and his position as Minister
of Education in 1956, had made him a threat to the
leader of the Party, Gheorghiu-Dej. The appointment of Miron Constantinescu as the Minister of
Education in 1969, was a symbol of a 'new age' in
Romanian education; a new system that was to be
reflective of traditional Romanian education from

before the war period which was to be geared
totally to Romania and Romania's needs and aspir-
ations.[45]

The reform of 1968[46] is summed up in an official publication as follows:

The law of 1968, still in force, has operated
in several directions: extension of compulsory schooling from eight to ten years, extension and diversification of high school
education, change in the ratio of general
secondary schools and specialized schools in
favour of the latter, steady modernization of
curricula, textbooks, academic courses and
teaching methods.[47]

It was the Central Committee of the Communist Party in Romania that authorized the 1968 reform
which was called "The Law concerning Instruction
in Romania". In 1969, the Central Committee also
promulgated the document concerning "The Status
of Faculty in Romania".[48] This document which had
the force of law, laid down the rules for the
training of teachers, their appointment, their
promotion and their in-service training which
would be under the auspices of the Institute for
the Perfecting of Teaching Faculty. The latter
was responsible for the teacher's particular sub-
ject-matter, for methodology and also for the continuing training of the teacher in ideology.

Section 2: The Contemporary Structure

Pre-School Education: This includes nurser-
ies and kindergarten in Romania, but primarily
kindergarten. All schools in Romania are co-edu-
cational. Pre-school education is not compulsory
in Romania, but began to get special attention in
1971 with the establishment of a special committee
dealing with kindergarten at the Ministry of Education. In 1973, 45.7% of the total age-group attended Kindergarten, and the projection for the
early '80's was that over 80% of all children
would attend Kindergarten.[49] One of the most im-

54

portant missions of the Kindergarten is to train
children in the intellectual skills needed for
the Grade Schools.[50] Teachers in Kindergarten
are trained in special 5-year High Schools but
some of the older teachers have no special training. Some of the teachers are products of 2 or
3-year Pedagogical Institutes. There are also
some University graduates teaching in Kindergartens.

Grade School: The reform of 1968 increased
the compulsory school period to ten years so that
after eight grades, there begins a diversity in
the type of schooling for the two remaining years
of compulsory education. The general structure at
present in Romania is:
(a). Grades I-IV, which has a general program.
The faculty are usually products of 3-year Pedagogical Institutes, not University, although the
training of teachers for I-IV is now in a process
of change. Children start school at the age of
six.
(b). Grades V-VIII, become more specialized, with
some students already starting to learn trades.
In Grade V, foreign language study also begins,
although some Kindergarten and Grades I-IV are also now beginning specialization in languages.
Teachers for these grades are trained in the University, but some of the teachers, usually in
Grades V-VI, are trained in 3-year Pedagogical Institutes.

Grades I-VIII, are still in the same building
usually, but the development program in education
which took place in 1971-'73, is attempting to
unify in some form, Grades I-X, the compulsory
period of education. In my research design, I
treated Grades I-VIII as a continuous unit, called
Grade School, in keeping with the structure of the
institutions where I did the research.

High School: High School is now undergoing
an extensive process of change because of the introduction of the ten year compulsory period. But
in general, there is the academic-type High School

55

which can be devoted to the real sciences or the
humanities. Some of the academic-type High
Schools concentrate on music or economics, for
example, or a particular foreign language. In
general these are the University track High
Schools, in the sense that students from these
schools make up the majority of University entrants.[51]

Then there are the high schools that special-
ize but whose graduates go primarily into the work
force, or who are trained as sub-engineers or
foremen for example. These are the Specialized
High Schools. In the school year 1972-1973, the
table for this type of school was as follows:[52]

Industrial	High Schools:	47.4%
Agricultural	High Schools:	18.4%
Economic	High Schools:	17.4%
Pedagogical	High Schools:	15.1%
Health	High Schools:	1.00%
Silviculture	High Schools:	0.70%

The ratio between the high schools of real sciences
and humanities and the Specialized High Schools
over three academic years was as follows:

	High Schools of Real Sciences & Humanities	Specialized High Schools
1971-72	2	1
1972-73	1.5	1
1973-74	1.02	1

In general, the Government of Romania is
trying to move the whole educational system into a
track in line with the acquisition of skills directly relevant to production. Only University
graduates can teach in the High Schools.

Vocational & Technical Schools: One hundred

and fifty-three specialities are dealt with in
these schools which also show a great variety in
training and methodology, ranging from the theoretical to the very practical. Vocational and
technical schools also show great variety in the
period of training. I did not do research in
this type of school.

Higher Education: There are Universities,
Academies, Institutes, and Conservatories. There
are six universities in Romania, with nineteen
university centers. The general undergraduate
education takes four years. The Academy is for
the study of economics and politics, in general
preparing students for work in production and administration of production, and for the special
position of ideological cadres within the administrative structure of the Communist Party. The
Institutes may cover fields from the technical to
the artistic. The conservatories are for music.
There is also the Academy of the Socialist Republic of Romania which was intended in general as
an organization for the outstanding figures in
science and letters. It still has to some extent
this function, but it has become gradually also an
area of special attention by the Party, with the
appointment of figures who are distinguished for
their Party function rather than for their learning.[53] The Academy maintains an extensive series
of Institutes ranging from literary and linguistic
studies to real science. Some of the researchers
in these Institutes are pursuing doctoral studies
while others pursue pure research or research
linked with production.

My observation and participant observation in
Higher Education was done in the university structure. However, researchers in the Institutes of
the Academy, as well as Academicians were interviewed, because of their importance in the educational and intellectual life of Romanian society.
They often produce the primary materials that
teachers and professors use; they also sit on education committees on the national level.

In general it can be said about education in
Romania that education, literacy, and culture
have a high place in the hierarchy of values in
Romanian society. Freshmen for example, come to
the University with an extensive knowledge of
world literature, art, and music. The educated
man in Romania is a man who is highly literate,
highly cultured in the German sense of 'kultur',
and who has a University degree.

It is difficult to chart the contemporary
system of education in Romania in clear and unam-
biguous tables. The '70's are a period of reorganization of the whole educational system. It
is not yet clear whether one particular structure
will emerge. But in general it can be said that
there is a general tendency, which was evidenced
throughout the research period, of using the concept of 'integration' as the principle or reorganization: the education should be linked as closely
as possible with work-experience and production;
that the trilogy of learning-work-ideology should
become a unit in Romania's drive towards modernization and multilateral development. These goals
involve moving from the humanities to subjects
which have an obvious link with production; moving
in general from the theoretical to the practical;
moving out from the classroom into the life of
work and production. There was also a growing
tendency to increase, especially in the various
institutions of Higher Learning, the time spent in
ideological training, both directly in the classroom and through the various organizations which
have an ideological purpose for their existence.
In a series of interviews with ten professors at
the end of my research in April-June, 1976, it was
said that the President felt that ideological com-
mitment by the intellectual elite in the country
was word-deep; that there would be an increase of
ideological training in the university, of the
direct and indirect kind, until ideological training would have a 1:1 ratio with professional
training.

NOTES

1. 'Roumania', 'Rumania', and 'Romania' is the evolution of the spelling of the name of the country in English. "The Romanians are the only Romance people to have preserved their ethnic name; the adjective roman from the Latin form romanus and the noun romani from the Latin romani." D. Macrea, "Latinity of the Romanian Language and its Specific Evolution", Romanian Bulletin, Vol. 6, no. 6 (June, 1977), p. 9.

2. Tiberiu-Morariu et al., The Geography of Romania, 2nd ed., (Bucharest: Meridiane Publishing House, 1969), p. 9.

3. Abraham Melezin, "The Land", in Romania, Stephen Fischer-Galati (New York: Praeger, 1957), p. 14.

4. David Floyd, Rumania (New York: Praeger, 1965), p. 2.

5. Romania Yearbook 1975 (Bucharest: Editura Stintifica si Enciclopedica, 1975), p. 12.

6. For further discussion on Romania's borders, see: Julian Hale, Ceausescu's Romania: A Political Documentary (London: George G. Harrap & Co. Ltd., 1971), pp. 24-44.

7. Field Notes, October, 1973.

8. Romania, 2nd ed. (Bucharest: Meridiane Publishing House, 1971), p. 89.

9. Ibid., p. 92.

10. Republica Socialista Romania, Directia Centrala de Statistica, Recensamintul Populatiei si Locuintilor din 15 Martie 1966, Bucuresti, 1969.

11. For a detailed discussion of minorities in

Romania, see: Gilberg Trond, "Ethnic Minorities in Romania under Socialism", in East European Quarterly (Jan., 1974), pp. 435-464.

12. When I suggested in the Institute of Linguistics, a research institute attached to the Academy of Romania, some problems for research in the area of sociolinguistics dealing with social bilingualism among minorities in June, 1974, I was greeted with laughter. In general all research that potentially explores any social differences is taboo in Romania.

13. Romania (1971), p. 82.

14. Gilberg Trond, Modernization in Romania since World War II (New York: Praeger, 1975), p. 34. Hereafter called "Modernization".

15. Field Notes, December, 1973 and April, 1975.

16. The results of this drive can be seen already. In the November 20, 1977 elections in Romania for the People's Councils, 33% of the elected deputies are under 35 and 35% of the deputies elected were women. Romanian Bulletin, Vol. VII, no. 1, (Jan., 1978), p. 2.

17. From interviews with a random sample of both male and female University students in the calendar years 1974 and 1975 from three departments. Field Notes, September, 1974 to May, 1975.

18. The information in this paragraph was gathered in the 1971-1973 period of the research.

19. Nicolae Ceausescu, Report at the National Conference of the RCP, July 19-21, 1972 (Bucharest: Meridiane Publishing House, 1972), p. 96.

20. In the period 1971-1976, there were three inspections, each lasting 2-3 weeks, by an al-

ternate member of the Executive Committee of
the Central Committee of the RCP in the department of the University where I did the
focal research on the University level.
This involved general observation, attendance at classes, interviewing faculty and
students, attendance at Party, Union, and
Faculty meetings, attendance at all student
meetings, attendance at the Dean's Council
meetings, inspection of books and materials
used in courses in the department.

21. Usually in Communist societies, the official
    Party ideologue, for example, Suslov in the
    USSR today, is not also the official Party
    or State leader.

22. For official literature, almost any book pub-
    lished in Romania on any subject, fiction ex-
    cluded, will contain numerous references to
    Ceausescu; for an example of an official ver-
    sion published in Switzerland, see: La
    Roumanie economique et culturelle. Geneve:
    Librairie Droz, 1970. For non-official lit-
    erature, see: Stan Newens, Nicolae Ceausescu.
    Nottingham, England: The Bertrand Russell
    Peace Foundation, 1972. Michel-P. Hamelet,
    Nicolae Ceausescu. Paris: Seghers, 1971.
    Kenneth Jowitt, Revolutionary Breakthroughs
    and National Development. Berkeley & Los
    Angeles: University of CAlifornia Press,
    1971.

23. Ion Ratiu, Contemporary Romania (Richmond,
    England: Foreign Affairs Publishing Co. Ltd.,
    1975), pp. 69-71 and pp. 103-107.

    Julian Hale, op. cit., pp. 92-3.

24. Gilberg Trond, Modernization, p. 88.

25. For the historical development of the UCY,
    see: Constantin Barbulescu et al., File din
    Istoria U.T.C. Bucuresti: Editura Politica,
    1971. For the general philosophy and struc-

ture of the UCY, see: Ion Iliescu's report
to UCY IXth Congress in Romania's Youth.
Bucharest: Meridiane Publishing House, 1971.

26. For example, Ion Iliescu (see: n. 25 above),
was Secretary General of the UCY until 1971.
He was then over 40, and an alternate member
of the Executive Committee of the Central
Committee of the RCP. He later became a
Central Committee secretary in 1971. The
Party structure and hierarchy pay special attention to the UCY. The President himself
had been in charge of the UCY in 1940 and
throughout his early career was closely involved with ideological training and assessment; he had also been involved in the military in this function. From interviews with
a group of teachers: Field Notes, July, 1975.

27. The Romania Yearbook 1975, p. 17, tells us
that Romania is divided administratively as
follows: "Administrative Divisions: 39
Counties, 236 towns (47 of them are municipalities, Bucharest municipality having the
regime of a county) and 2,706 communes
(13,149 villages)." Bucharest, the capital,
where I did my research has then the status
of a county.

28. For example, in the elections mentioned above
in no. 16, of deputies elected to the People's Councils, only "24% of them are not
Party members, they are enrolled in other organizations of the Socialist Unity Front".
Romanian Bulletin, Vol. VII, no. 1. (Jan.,
1978), p. 2.

29. For some of the ideas behind the Pioneer movement in Romania, see the following by a
Deputy Minister of Education: Vigiliu Radu-
lian, "Directions and Perspectives in the
Activities of the Pioneers' Organizations in
the Socialist Republic of Romania", in
National Symposium. Bucharest, 23-24 May,
1969 (No publisher or date of publication

included).

30. Nicolae Ceausescu, Cuvintul, Gazeta Invata-mintuliu, November 15, 1966, p. 1.

31. Gilberg Trond, Modernization, pp. 81-2.

32. See: Romanian Bulletin, Vol. VII, no. 1 (Jan., 1978), p. 1.

33. Economic Development in Communist Romania (Cambridge, Mass.: The M.I.T. Press, 1967), p. 1.

34. Gilberg Trond, Modernization, pp. 141-2.

35. Ibid., p. 150.

36. David Turnock, An Economic Geography of Roma-nia (London: G. Bell & Sons Ltd., 1974), p. 203.

37. Gilberg Trond, Modernization, p. 152.

38. For a detailed discussion of this period in Romania, see: Ghita Ionescu, The Reluctant Ally (London: Ampersand Ltd., 1965), pp. 33-106.

39. For the reform in education in Romania in 1948, see: Ghita Ionescu, Communism in Roma-nia 1944-1962 (London: Oxford University Press, 1964), pp. 173-75. For the anti-communist viewpoint, see: The Perversion of Education in Romania. Washington, D. C.: Ruma-nian National Committee, 1950. For each official position, see: The Rumanian Review, 1949 (no. 1, p. 17-22; nos. 3-4, pp. 23-48); 1950, no. 6, pp. 5-12. This Review is a very important source to see the evolution in thought officially in Romania from Vol. 1, May, 1946 to the Volumes in 1949, from pro-Western, pro-Soviet in 1946 to bitter anti-Westernism in 1949 when Romania becomes almost identified with the USSR. For pre-1948

and post-1948 education in Romania see:
Joseph S. Roucek and Kenneth V. Lottich,
Behind the Iron Curtain (Caldwell, Idaho:
The Caxton Printers, Ltd., 1964), pp. 304ff.
This book and the following are decidedly
anti-communist, but they give a picture of
the 1946-1950 period in Romania, with some
documentation, that is otherwise unavailable.
See: Reuben H. Markham, Rumania under the
Soviet Yoke. Boston: Meador Publishing Com-
pany, 1949.

40. "According to the census of October 1945,
there were some 4 million illiterates in a
population of approximately 15 million."
Education in the Socialist Republic of Roma-
nai (Bucharest: Ministry of Education, 1973),
p. 8. Romania's program of the eradication
of illiteracy resulted in the announcement
by the Government in 1958 that illiteracy
had been abolished.

41. For the period March 1953-February 1956, see:
Ghita Ionescu, Communism, pp. 219-54.

42. Ibid., pp. 241-47.

43. Most works dealing with Romania published after '69, stress the de-Sovietization of Romania in the '60's and tell the story of the
renaming of the Gorky Institute. But the renaming is only half the story; there is
another more symbolic part: in the entrance
hall of this Institute of Foreign Languages
there is a statue; it used to be in pre-'48,
the Virgin. She lost her head and part of
her top; a bust of Gorky was superimposed on
the quasi-asexual section of the statue of
the Virgin. Gorky lost his head in the de-
Sovietization period in Romania to be replaced by Romania's National poet, Eminescu;
the bottom half of the statue is still the
sculptured robe of the Virgin.

44. For the reform of 1968, see: Randolph L.

Braham, Education in Romania (Washington, D.
C.: US Gov't. Printing Office, 1972), pp. 13-
17.

45. For the career and brief biography of Miron
Constantinescu, see: Ghita Ionescu, Communism, pp. 284-7, and pp. 351-2.

46. For an official discussion of the reforms of
1968, see: Le mouvement educatif dans la
Republique Socialiste de Roumanie pendant
l'annee scolaire 1967-1968. Bucharest:
Editions Didactique et Pedagogique, 1968.

47. Education in the SRR (1973), p. 9.

48. Dumitru Muster and George Vaideanu, "Romania:
Contemporary Romanian Education" in Journal
of Education Vol. 152, (February, 1970), p.
65.

49. Education in the SRR (1973), p. 17.

50. Field Notes, October, 1972. The interviewee
is an official from the Ministry of Education,
responsible for Kindergarten education.

51. In a survey done in three departments of the
University, with a random sample of students
that was just over 30% of the population,
there were no entrants among the freshmen in
either 1974 or 1975, who were from High
Schools other than High Schools of real
sciences and humanities. Field Notes, October, 1974; October 1975.

52. Education in SRR (1973), pp. 25-30.

53. From interviews with five members of the Academy of the SRR in the period 1973-1976. It
was also said that the President did not look
favorably on the Academy because of: their
special privileges that were not a direct result of Party or State hierarchical status;
their general pre-regime bourgeois standing;

their structural independence from direct Party control (there is, however, intense Party control), and their general independence (as distinct from other institutions in Romanian society). In the period of the research, 1971-'76, there was a general cutback in the academic activities of the Academy, with the abolition also of certain research facilities and Institutes that were under the governance of the Academy. The President's wife is the Director of one of the research Institutes of the Academy, the Institute of chemical research.

CHAPTER III

AN HISTORICAL PERSPECTIVE

In <u>Romania's Ceausescu</u>, Donald Catchlove says: "In Romania, history is everything".[1]   In the contemporary ideological training in Romania, items from Romania's history are presented as part of the ideology. In this chapter, I am presenting those aspects of Romania's history which form part of the ideology today. This will eliminate constant historical references that would otherwise be necessary as explanation. For example, the reference in the ideological training to the latinity of the Romanian language must be understood in its historical context. Otherwise it makes little sense.

I am dividing up the historical references into three parts. The first part will deal with the ethnic origins of Romania. The second part will deal with the domination of Romania by foreign powers and Romania's striving to assert its independence. The second part will also include Romania's territorial claims. The third part will deal with the history of modern Romania, including the occupation of Romania in 1944 by Soviet troops, and the forming of a Communist regime in the period after 1944. The approach here is selective, both in method and in content. The content I include is only the content relevant to my study of the contemporary ideological training. The method I use is, for the most part, sociological. I view history as the Romanians view their history.

I will use material from my field notes gathered from both observation and interview. I will also use printed material as documentation to fill out the gaps in the history when this is necessary for a fuller understanding. Sometimes I will use my own words to summarize events and attitudes, as told to me by Romanians.

Part I: Romania's Ethnic Origins

Until the end of the first century, the in-
habitants of Romania were the Dacians. They were
colonized by the Romans. In the period of coloni-
zation, they lost their language. Through intermarriage with the Romans, a new ethnic people e-
merged, the Daco-Romans.

When the Romans near the end of the first
century A.D., under the Emperor Trojan, expanded
eastwards, they had to wage war with the Dacians,
who inhabited the territory north of the Danube.
The Dacians, under Decebal, inflicted many defeats
on the Romans even exacting tribute from them, but
after the second campaign in 105-6 A.D. the Romans
finally defeated and colonized the local population. This historical event becomes a lesson, for
example, in the kindergarten.[2]

The reason for the importance of this event
is two-fold. In answer to the question: "Why is
the Roman occupation a matter of pride for Romanians?", the answer was almost invariably the
same: 'Transylvania is Romanian, it belonged to
the Dacians, then to the Daco-Romans, the fore-
fathers of the Romanian nation.'[3]

The territory of Transylvania has been a territory disputed for hundreds of years between the
Romanians and the Hungarians. The Romanian government, Romanian historians and archeologists
spent a lot of time and money trying to prove that
Transylvania was Daco-Roman: that when the Romans
evacuated the province of Dacia felix under the
Emperor Aurelian in the third century because of
pressure from the invading tribes, the withdrawal
was purely military. The local population had already adopted the Latin language. There had been
frequent intermarriage. The intermarriage of the
Dacians and the Romans produced a new ethnic group
called the Daco-Romans. These Daco-Romans are the
ancestors of the Romanian people. The terms 'Daco-
Roman' and 'Romanian' are often used interchange-
ably in the ideological training.

In one kindergarten class, the following was said: 'Decebal was the first hero of the Romanian people. He defended Transylvania against the Roman armies, making some of them his slaves. When the Roman army, with help from all over Europe, finally occupied Romania, the Romans and the Dacians became friends. They became one people, the Daco-Romans. Decebal was such a great hero that the Roman Emperor gave him an honored place on the Trojan column.'[4] The teacher had a picture of Trojan's column, which she held up to the children. She then passed it around the class for the children to see close-up.

In another class, in the fourth year of primary school, the teacher said that 'the Dacians were never enslaved by the Romans. The Romans appreciated the advanced culture of the Dacians. The Romans stayed in Dacia as friends. The Dacians took from the Romans the Latin language, laws, and institutions. The Romans adopted from the Dacians their culture and civilization. At the end of the second century the two peoples had become one people.'[5]

At patriotic demonstrations, poems in honor of Decebal are frequently recited. The present leader of Romania is sometimes called the new Decebal at popular demonstrations. A feature film, the Dacians, stresses the great courage shown by Decebal and the Dacians. Two things are stressed in the schools: the bravery of the Daco-Romanian resistance to the Roman armies and the Romanization of the Dacians by the same armies.

In an interview, one of the foremost Romanian historians put it like this:

Romania is a geographical anomaly. Because of our position, the last country before you cross the Black Sea dividing Europe and Asia, we are always in the path of whoever wanted to cross, the Roman armies, the barbaric tribes, the Turks, the Cossacks, The Austrian Empire, the Russians. We are surrounded on all sides by

Slavs and Huns, who, if they want to grow
fatter, stretch into us. Understand me, I
am not against the Slavs and the Huns, but
remember somewhere they are all brothers; if
they want to stretch their paws they can find
us the non-Slavs. We belong culturally to
Europe, to French and German culture. Our
language is a Romance language, acquired
historically in the same way French was. Our
young people today are now adapting to the
culture of the English-language world, English
theater, American music, American literature,
American film and television. It may not be
very politic, but in our culture and our as-
pirations, we are westerners. My generation
look to France, the young now look to the
dominant Western culture. We are a people
caught in a . . . . like a schizophrenia,
geographically in the East, but in 'soul' we
belong to the West.[6]

In the follow-up question I asked: "But Professor,
why stress that you were conquered by the Romans,
being conquered is not something people boast a-
bout?"

This is our lifeline to the West. We are
Western by blood, by language, by civilization. Maybe you know, that the Hungarians
also claim Transylvania. Transylvania was
Dacian; the Romans were mixed with Dacian
blood. Transylvania is ours, with our people
living there since the time of our ancestors,
the Dacians . . . an unbroken heritage that
continued after the collapse of the Roman Empire. Do you think the Dacians vanished into
the waters of the Danube? All the evidence
is there, in archaeological findings, in to-
ponymy. Read the books in English and French
if you like, Foting, Dissesco, Seton-Watson,
Ghyka, Ifor-Evans.[7]

In a later interview, I was also given the works
of Romanian writers, some contemporary and some
from the last century who emphasized the Latinity

of the Romanian people.[8] The reading of all these
books formed the basis for future discussions and
interviews with Romanian academicians and professors. These books were also the primary sources
for many of the lessons I observed in kindergarten, primary school, high school and in university
and in social evenings of patriotic speeches,
poems and songs, which included reference to the
continuing Roman patrimony of Romania, in race,
culture, and language.

An older high school teacher in an interview
about the romanization of Romania, said:

You will never know what it meant after '44,
when we had to lie to our children in the
schools when with the rest of the lies, we had
to tell them that Romania was under the influence of the Slavs since before the Romans,
that the Slavs were always our friends. We
had to forget everything we ever learned in
school from the great Romanian historians[9]
like Hurmuzaki. These Cossacks and Huns
weren't satisfied with stealing everything
we had, and treating us like gypsies, but we
had to tell our children lies, that the Slavs[10]
had always been our ancestors.

The Romanian teachers whom I interviewed, who
had been teachers or students in the '50's, confirmed this. A university professor gave me cop-
ies of the two official histories of Romania from
the fifties.[11] These virtually omit the Roman influence, with the accent on Slavic development and
stability in the first centuries of 'our era'.
The same professor told me:

We all wrote those books. They didn't put our
names on them because some of us had books
that had been published during the war itself
that said the opposite of what was in the new
ones. We had to write them, to prove our
loyalty to the new regime. We had supervisors, Russians and 'Romanian working class'
who told us in general what should be said.

71

The Romanian learns quickly. But you don't
know. Whether I say the Daco-Romans stayed
in Romania after the evacuation of the Roman
garrisons does not change the truth. Our
people knew the truth. They knew that we
had to do it if we were going to eat, to
drink, to make love, to keep the nation going.
Every Romanian was under the yoke. Some gave
them grain and oil, we only gave them printed
lies after all and everyone knew they were
lies.[12]

One professor who had contributed in 1952, to
the Slavic-Soviet-Russian oriented official history of Romania, Istoria R.P.R., very proudly gave
me a book published in America that deals in some
depth with the re-writing of history in Romania in
the late '40's and '50's.[13] In this book, Michael
J. Rura divides the re-writing into: reinterpretation by omission, substitution, emphasis, and cor-
ruption. The period of Romanian history, 1947-'54,
when the historians and writers were so strictly
controlled that they had to write to order, is
called by Ghita Ionescu, the "Roller Period".
This was when Mihail Roller was in charge of the
section in Agitprop[14] dealing with "revising Romanian historiography in general and history text-
books in particular."[15]

Some professors interviewed put the blame for
the falsification of Romanian history in the '50's
on the fact that 'Chisinevschi, Rautu, and Roller
were not Romanians . . . but Bessarabians, Russian
citizens, Jews; they perform for any master. We
still have the same type pretending now they're
loyal patriotic Romanians.'[16] I mention this because, as we will see later, many of the interviewed stressed that the political ideology today
is a foreign import.

However, since the '60's, the official history of the Romanization of the Dacians is now
non-Slavic oriented. Officially, Decebal has been
reinstored as a Romanian hero; Transylvania was
romanized; the Romanians never abandoned their

72

country; the language of the Romanians is again said to be more Latin than modern Italian. This patriotic and nationalistic turnabout started with the relaxation of Sovietization that took place after the death of Stalin.

For years everything to do with the bourgeois past had been neglected. Suddenly everything changed. Statues were cleaned and buildings of historical interest were repainted. From about this time, early in 1967, similar changes succeeded one another in such profusion and so quickly that people could hardly believe that it was happening. Visits to various parts of the country by Party leaders, headed by Ceausescu and Maurer, were frequent and the ceremonial elaborate. The motorcade would be received at the city gates by the local officials flanked by 30 or so young people in national costume. A silver key of the city would be presented to Ceausescu on a velvet cushion: also a platter of bread and salt, the way Voevods of old were received.[17]

Romania, with its Roman heritage has again become the target of official teaching in the fostering of nationalism and patriotism, not Russia and Slavism as in the early days of communist rule in Romania in the late '40's and early '50's. This oscillation in the targeting of patriotism and nationalism is illustrative of the difficulty faculty have in presenting official ideology in the schools and universities. One high school teacher can speak for more than fifty teachers and professors who made a similar point about ideological training:

I finished high school in 1949, then I went to the university for five years. Stalin was the God and Russia was our saviour. Romania was nothing, the Slav was everything. Now, Romania is the best in the world, we are Latins again. I am happy we are Romanians again. But what about tomorrow, maybe we will be Russians again. If the Russians take more of

73

our land, give some more of it to the Bulgarians and Hungary is allowed to take Transylvania, what will I tell the pupils? Those
lands were never ours? Our leaders misled
us? You never know what you will be told to
say. There's a meeting, the Party Secretary
gets up, you're told there's a big change.
What do you do? 'I kiss your hand, Comrade', and you say what you are told to. Now
at least, we can tell them honestly about our
beautiful land, we can say some honest things
at least about our country, not everything
but something.[18]

In many interviews with students, teachers, and
professors there occurs this constant theme: you
never know from semester to semester what you
can't say today that you could say yesterday.
That today you must deny what you said was sacred
yesterday; you never know what you will have to
say tomorrow. Writers, artists, journalists and
many groups outside education confirm this summing-
up of the situation: facts can change, but obedience remains constant.

Part II: Romania's Domination by Foreign Powers
         and Her Struggle for Independence
Section 1: Romania's Domination by Foreign Powers

There is one central fact, which must never be
lost sight of if one wants to understand the
Romanians today: ever since they were established as a nation they lived united in one
and the same country for only one brief spell,
between 1 December 1918, and 17 June 1940 –
less than 22 years.[19]

Luckily, in talking about Romania's borders
as a nation, my purpose is sociological and not
historical. For my purpose the nation-state of Romania is geographically as Romanians interpret their nation-state. This includes
present-day Romania, plus Bessarabia and a section
of Bucovina, the parts of Moldavia that now form
part of the Soviet Union known as Moldavia S.S.R.

74

and that part of Southern Dobroja now under Bulgarian rule.

In many of the extended interviews with students and educators, the discussion came around to: if you want to understand what is going on in Romania, to understand the Romanian mentality, you must understand what it means to belong to a people who have been the plaything of foreign domination for almost all their history. The normal situation for the Romanian is to be told how to work and what to do. The present government in Romania is Romanian; it advocates Romanian patriotism and nationalism. The interviewees, however, said that the present rule is similar to foreign rule in this aspect: now, the same as always, we are told what to do, what we should do, what we can't do. We are told what to think, what to value and of course what to say.[20]

In the dominations of Romania by foreign powers, Romania sometimes had heroes who tried to defend the people from the oppressors, either by word or deed. Historical patriotism, as the guide-light for contemporary patriotism and nationalism, is an important part of contemporary ideological training in the Romanian schools: patriotism and nationalism are interpreted in the words and deeds of the historical defenders of Romania's freedom. Individual heroes are presented as the models for contemporary Romanian patriots.

Section 2: Romania's Struggle for Independence and Her Traditional Heroes

What follows is a very brief summary of Romanian history, highlighting the heroes now presented as models for Romanian students and for all Romanians. These model-heroes are presented in the ideological training in the schools, in stories, verse and drama, in the media, in films, in demonstrations, not simply as lessons in history but as ideological models. My treatment is again, historico-sociological. I am not implying that there is no serious study of history in Romanian schools;

but what follows is taken from observations of ideological training and demonstrations in schools.

1. In the third century, what is called Romania by Romanians was invaded by the migratory tribes such as the Goths and the Huns. Some of these tribes stayed a short whole and then moved elsewhere; those who stayed were assimilated with the local population. In the sixth and seventh centuries the Slavs came and were also assimilated; they introduced some Slavic terms into the Latin language of the Romanians and in place names.

2. After the eleventh century, the Hungarians who had migrated as barbaric tribes from the Urals started to settle in Transylvania on the lands of the Romanians who had been there before, during, and after the Romans, without temporal interruption; they brought in other people to settle in Transylvania, the Szeklers and the Saxon-Germans.²¹ The Hungarians, the Szeklers and the Saxons, each had a certain autonomy as a group, but the native Romanians on their own land were treated as servants and slaves. Many Romanians found refuge in the mountains as shepherds; for this reason the sheep-herding folk-lore is given great prominence in Romanian life today. The epic poem, Miorita (The Lamb), is regarded by Romanians as the most loved and the most Romanian of all pieces of literature in their language.

3. Wallachia and Moldavia and Dobroja are the other states or regions that make up Romania. The first ruler of Wallachia who is now presented as a Romanian hero is Basarab (The First). Bogdan (The First), also in the fourteenth century, is the first hero-ruler of Moldavia. They are mentioned in contemporary films, poetry, drama as the archetypal patriots, the patriarchs of patriotism.

4. When the Turks started to expand their empire, various Romanian rulers heriocally defended their territories against them. Mircea cel Batrin, (The Old), the ruler of Wallachia, halted the

Turks. Iancu de Hunedoara, the voivod of Transylvania, defeated the Turks. Vlad Tepes (The Impaler), the ruler of Wallachia, fought against the Turks successfully.[22] After Vlad's death, at the end of the fifteenth century, Wallachia came under Turkish sovereignty, with the Sultan appointing the rulers. In the meantime, in Moldavia, Stefan cel Mare (Stephen The Great) was successful against the Turks, driving them out of power in Wallachia and replacing the Sultan's appointed ruler with a loyal Romanian. Stefan cel Mare was a man of culture, founding monasteries of beautiful architecture and artistic merit. When he died in 1504, Moldavia and Wallachia became slave states of the Turks. Transylvania, even after the Turks had defeated the Hungarian Kingdom, remained independent of Hungary and of the Turks. The Romanian peasants also revolted against the Hungarian **boieri** (nobles and landlords) in Transylvania, and were savagely repressed.

5. At the end of the sixteenth century, Mihai Viteazul (Michael The Brave or The Swift), ruler of Wallachia, rose against the Turks. He also crossed into Transylvania, defeating the Hungarian prince. Mihai Viteazul, in 1600 at Alba-Iulia, declared himself the ruler of Wallachia, Moldavia and Transylvania, the first time the three principalities were united under one Romanian ruler.

6. In the next century, many Greeks came to the principalities, with one family becoming pro-Romanian ruler of Wallachia; some members of this family were Serban Cantacuzino and Canstantin Brincoveanu. In Moldavia, the Romanian scholar and hero, Dimitrie Cantemir, tried to free Romania from the Turks. The Turks decided to put only Greeks, generally called the Phanariot (Greeks), on the thrones of Wallachia and Moldavia. From early in the eighteenth century onwards, Transylvania was becoming the meeting ground for battle between the Turks and the Austrians.

7. In the mountains of Apuseni, in Transylvania, the Romanian peasants, led by Horia, Closca,

77

and Crisan, revolted against the nobles in the
fight to abolish serfdom. The brutality of the
nobles in putting down the revolt was worse than
ever witnessed in Romania under the Turks. Horia
and Closca were murdered on the wheel.

8. Early in the nineteenth century, the Romanian peasant, Tudor Vladimerescu, marched in a
popular uprising from Oltenia to Bucharest, drawing crowds of patriots with him. He was murdered
under orders of the Phanariot Greek rulers. In
the 1820's and '30's the Turks began to yield to
the Russians in the areas of Wallachia and Moldavia.

9. The revolutionary writers who were also
historians, Mihail Kogalniceanu in Moldavia and
Nicolae Balcescu in Wallachia, tried to organize
a social revolution in 1848. The Turks were called in by the Romanian rulers who had regained
favor in the eyes of the Sultan. The revolution
was crushed. In 1848, the Romanian peasants in
Transylvania started to organize under Avram
Iancu, to gain independence for Transylvania and
union with Wallachia and Moldavia.²³

10. In spite of world opposition, Alexandru
Ioan Cuza became the ruler of both Wallachia and
Moldavia in 1859. This signalled the end of feudalism and the real beginnings of education in
Romania. However, Cuza was replaced because of
world protest. In his place was established a
foreign prince who was acceptable to the world
powers, Prince Carol of Hohenzollern-Sigmaringen.

Section 3: Change in Attitude towards the Tradi-
          tional Heroes: Two Stages since the Ad-
          vent of the Communist Regime in Romania

     In the early years of Communist rule in Roma-
nia, when the Marx-Engels-Lenin-Stalin philosophy
of history²⁴ was adopted as the basis of Romanian
history, only one of the Romanian historical
heroes was saved condemnation in the new histories
that were to serve as the basis for all instruc-

78

tion in Romania.

Of all the princes who figure in the relatively brief communist exposition on this subject, Stephen the Great is unique in that he has earned some Communist praise, this attributable to his relations with the Russians and his hostile attitude toward certain boyars.[25]

However, in the contemporary period, which can conveniently be called 'The Ceausescu Period', not only are the heroes presented as models, as we have already seen, but the President himself, is pictured as the 'reincarnation' of Stefan and Mihai.[26]

The official attitude to Romania's heroes changed drastically from the '50's to the '60's. A professor who was responsible for teacher training in the '50's had this to say about the change in official attitude:

It was in 1952, at a meeting for the reorientation of High School teachers, a lady, from the regions of Maramures by her accent, that's the place that you find the true Romanian peasant where they suffered under the Hungarians for being Romanians, said to me after a six hour meeting of speeches, 'Will I go back now and tell my children that Mihai Viteazul, the Greatest Romanian, was the son of a barman, that he made slaves of the peasants and that all his brave soldiers who fought for the unification of our country were foreigners, mercenaries?' Friend, what would you think of a government that made you tell your students that all the Irish heroes who gave their lives for Ireland were anti-Irish and only the people who helped England were true heroes? Times have changed now, Mihai was made clean again. But if they told us to say those things, how could we believe anything they said. Lies, my friend, became our daily bread, and we tell plenty of them now too, but we do not have to spit on Mihai anymore.[27]

In many of the interviews with educators and writers, the Romanian was explained to me in the context of the historical situation of exploitation. The Romanian has hardly ever been master in his own land. When the Romanian says negative things about the Romanian character, the reason for the negativeness is said to be the history of a people who have been ruled by foreign exploitation throughout most of their history. The contemporary centralization of control and rule by mobilization is also explained in terms of foreign exploitation: the Romanian is an expert at survival under the terms of mobilization.

Part III: The History of Modern Romania
Section 1: From 1881 to 1944

There are three possible sources for this period in Romanian history. Firstly, there is the official Communist version, which may change radically even in a short period of time. The official Communist version will also differ in the Romanian and Soviet versions. Secondly, there is the non-official scholarly version, as in Ghita Ionescu's Communism in Romania, 1944-62.[28] Thirdly, and perhaps more importantly for this study, there is the memory recall version of the teachers, professors, and academicians who were interviewed, including their reactions to the contemporary official version as presented in the schools. There is also the student version. The students learn about the period from the school and from other non-official sources such as the home. In general, it can be said, that while the contemporary ideological training in the schools, with regard to some of the history before the modern period has now come into line with the traditional approach of Romanian historians from before '44, especially in the nationalistic and patriotic aspects, the official treatment of the modern and contemporary period is very selective.[29] It omits periods, events and personalities, including communist figures who are dominant from 1940-1950. It frequent-

80

ly changes the nature of, and its attitude to, historical fact and personalities. Students and young educators are acutely aware of this kind of vacillation which becomes frequently the butt for jokes. The jokes also speculate on important contemporary figures and their treatment in history based on the model of contemporary official history.

The Kingdom of Romania was established in 1881, with King Carol as the first monarch. Peasant troubles began almost immediately, culminating in the peasant revolt in 1907. In one Grade School class that I visited, this revolt was the subject of the ideological lesson of the day, with the emphasis on the exploitation of the peasants by the capitalists.[30] At the end of World War I, Romania was made politically larger than it has ever been in history. It lost some of this territory again at the beginning of World War II, but gained some of it back at the end of the war.

"The Communist Party of Romania, section of the Communist International" was founded in Romania in 1921.[31] Much of the membership was Hungarian and Jewish, from the regions which came under Romanian rule after World War I.[32] The Moscow-based Comintern, which was the Soviet organization attached to their foreign affairs department to direct Communist Parties in other countries, instructed the Romanian Communist Party in the '20's to oppose the Romanian government; to petition for the giving up by Romania of Transylvania and Bessarabia which had joined Romania voluntarily at the end of World War I. The joining of Transylvania and Bessarabia with Romania had been ratified internationally at the Treaty of Saint-Germain in September, 1919.[33] The Communist Party was banned in Romania in 1924; "to most Romanians, the Communist Party represented an alien force working for the disintegration of their country."[34]

In the period before the war, 1939-1945, there was a significant fascist movement in Romania which was banned at various times and reappeared

under different names. It was called at various
times, The League of the Archangel Michael: The
Iron Guard: The All-for-the-Fatherland Party.
Fascism had significant influence among the youth,
among both the working youth and the student population.[35] A University professor, who had a position of responsibility in the ideological training
of university students in Bucharest in 1975, said
to me in an interview:

> We are very watchful of the students in their
> behavior and in their ideas, because before
> the war and during it, many of the student
> leaders were fascists. The gypsy does not be-
> come a townsman in a day.[36]

The fascist group in Romania was not representative of Romania as a whole, but it became important when the fascists officially became part
of the Romanian government that had the approval
of the Nazis in 1940.

On August 23, 1939, "Article 3 of the secret
additional protocol of the Nazi-Soviet Pact of 23,
August, 1939,"[37] gave Bessarabia to the Soviet
Union, which they had first taken in 1812. The
cessation of Bessarabia to the Soviet Union was
supported by the Romanian Communist Party. Romania is still without the territory of Bessarabia.
In the interviews about political ideology, many
of the interviewed referred to this Nazi-Soviet
pact. As an example of a prevalent opinion, I
will quote the remarks of a professor-historian:

> Marxism and Communism are the luxury of you
> Western intellectuals for your seminar dis-
> cussions. It is the perrogative of the naive.
> I was amused when I heard of the notoriety a
> professor gains in California when he is cal-
> led a Marxist. In our part of the world, com-
> munism is power. The Russians would have
> stayed with Hitler if they hadn't realized
> that Hitler was coming for them too. Hitler
> gave Bessarabia as an appetizer to them, at
> our expense. The Romanians in Moldavia have

been banished all over the Soviet Union.
The Russians are not communists; they are
imperialists. We can now be independent and
patriotic, as long as we stay within the
lines set for us by Moscow; all that could
change tomorrow. I hope France will become
Communist, the young communists there deserve
the Russians.[38]

Many interviewees maintained that Russian expan-
sionism destroyed the chance of communism ever becoming a real entity in the minds of Romanians.

Hitler also gave Transylvania to the Hungarians and southern Dobroja to the Bulgarians to
win their support for the Axis cause. The Soviet
Union had not approved this action of Hitler. The
Romanian Communist Party, consequently, opposed
the action also.[39]

When the Romanian government joined with Germany in the invastion of the Soviet Union, Britain
declared war on Romania. Five days later, on
December 12, 1941, Romania declared war on the
U.S.A.

Romanian troops quickly captured Moldavian
Bessarabia and advanced further into the Soviet
Union. The Romanian, pro-German, Antonescu-gov-
ernment and its aggressiveness against the Soviet
Union, was heavily condemned in the '50's. The
Romanian participation on the part of the Nazis
was not emphasized in the period 1971-1976. Fascists are pictured as Germans primarily; it is only when the persecution of a 'communist hero',
like President Ceausescu himself, has to be emphasized, then the persecutors are sometimes portrayed as Romanians, but always as Fascist-Romanians.

The pro-German government in Romania was
overturned by a coup d'etat on August 23, 1944.
The responsibility for the coup is disputed by official and non-official historians.[40] The latter
say the King; the former say the Communist Party.
But the celebration of this coup by the contempo-

rary Communist government makes August 23 one of the sacred days in the Romanian communist year, with demonstrations and official celebrations. In the schools, this event is presented to the children and the students as a victory wrought for Romania by the Communist Party.

Section 2: Soviet Troops occupy Romania in 1944; a Communist Government is Formed in Romania

On August 31, 1944, Soviet tanks rolled into Bucharest. Soviet troops did not leave Romania until 1958. For the thirteenth time in two centuries Romania had been invaded by Russian troops, according to a non-communist Romanian writing about the event.[41] It is not called an invasion in official Communist history, but a liberation "from under the yoke of fascism", which is the phrase invariably used in the classroom, films, and the media. The Romanians now joined the Allied forces, and their behavior thereafter in the war in contemporary Romanian teaching in the schools and in the media, is presented as a glorious blow by Romania against fascism and nazism. This interpretation is agreed upon by non-communist historians.

In October, 1944, Winston Churchill said to Stalin: "So far as Britain and Russia are concerned, how would it do for you to have ninety per cent predominance in Roumania, for us to have ninety per cent of the say in Greece . . . . While this was being translated I wrote out on a half-sheet of paper:

Roumania:

Russia . . . 90%
Others . . . 10%[42]

Stalin agreed, and this beings the advent of a new regime in Romania, which is called in colloquial Romanian dupa patruzeci si patru, (Lit. 'after '44').

At Potsdam, when Churchill complaining "about
the position of British representatives in Bucharest, threw in Stalin's face the words: 'An iron
fence has come down around them.' . [43]. 'All
fairy-tales!' Stalin snapped back."

There begins now in Romania the process of
making Romania a communist country; in 1944, the
RCP had 1,000 members.[44] The government opposition was abolished, and the King abdicated on
December 30, 1947, stating in his abduction, "I
give the Romanian people the freedom to choose a
new form of State".[45]

I will now simply list the main points sum-
marizing what happened in Romania after '44: these
events are important as a factor that shaped contemporary reaction to ideological training. But
first I want to consider briefly a linguistic
problem. What term do I use, for example, to express that very soon after '44, there was established one-Party rule, because the opposition
parties were 'purged', 'eased out', 'neutralized',
'terrorized into submission', 'butchered', 're-
formed'? Or do I use the quasi-biblical 'There
came into being . . . .'? For pragmatic reasons,
I will summarize the events as they have been explained to me by Romanians, non-officially, who
now live in Romania. I am using interviews from a
cross-section of the people, both Party members
and non-party members; from the three sections of
the population, intellectuals, peasants, and workers that are officially recognized in Romania.
The information has been cross-checked in the interviews; I have also cross-checked with non-official and official references.

1. The political opposition was eliminated by
various means by the Communists. In the late '40's
and early '50's, high-ranking Communist Party members also were eliminated in the struggle for fac-
tional supremecy within the Party. However, there[46]
were never "educative trials" in Romania; no
communist was ever tried in public, and the trials
were military. The State executive and the judi-

85

ciary came under the total control of the communist Party, which was called the Romanian Workers Party from 1948 until the Contemporary Ceausescu period, when it is again called the Communist Party.

2. The new-regime government backed by the Soviet Union started to nationalize the industry and businesses of Romania. The land was divided, to be later collectivized.

3. Soviet-Romanian ('mixed') Companies, the Sovroms, were set up to include everything from cattle to oil. The Romanian share from these companies went to the Soviet Union in war damages and reparation.[47] There was starvation in Romania, some use the word famine, in a country renowned for its agricultural richness. The memory of the hunger is still alive and bitter because the situation was politically created.[48]

4. The Party membership increased rapidly after 1945. Everyone joined, including ex-Iron Guard members, security police from the pro-German government, Orthodox bishops and priests, teachers, professors, university students, politicians from former governments. That such enrollments were a farce was stressed in the plenary meeting of the Central Committee of December-January, 1961, by the leader of Romania, Gheorghe Gheorghiu-Dej.[49] This was the meeting when it was announced that many former 'comrades' had betrayed the Party in its organization of recruitment. The fast entry of hundreds of thousands of new members who rose to power with little or no ideological training was mentioned in interviews to me as the reason for the contemporary attitude on behalf of many Romanians towards ideology, politics, and Marxism in particular. The teachers of today who were students or teachers in the '50's were never politicized thoroughly. They had only rudimentary training in Communist ideology, as a result of which they could reproduce phrases. Hasty recruitment of Party members allowed entry without training or testing for committment.

5. Many Romanians told me that I could never
understand the Romanian attitude to political
authority today because I had never experienced
the fear of 'the knock at the door'. The fear of
the security forces is called 'the knock at the
door' from the late '40's and '50's. In the late
'40's and early '50's, the security forces would
knock at the door and take people to jail and the
camps. The study in depth of this period in Romania's history has never been published. In the
terror and the purges, many were killed or imprisoned. Punitive labor camps were set up. The
most well-known camp was the 'Canal' project,
Stalin's plan for a canal between the Black Sea
and the Danube which would give access by water
to Soviet troops through Romania and into Yugoslavia. There is now no 'terror' in Romania, but
the memory of the terror, the consciousness of the
omnipresence of the security police, real or im-
agined, is an important factor in the analysis of
the ideological training. One High School student
for example, read me a poem of his about the Canal, which for him belongs to the realm of cultural memory. The first line was:

"A river without water, flowing with putrid
flesh."

In the meeting of 1961, mentioned above, there was
a kind of apology for some of "the infamous frame-
ups" of this period by Dej.[50]

6. The Romanian Orthodox Church came under the
direction of the new government in 1948; dissent-
ers were eliminated. The Greek Uniate Church was
abolished. The Catholic Church was silenced.
Protestants, Jews, and Moslems were treated as
ethnic minorities rather than religious groups;
they could cooperate or be eliminated. Religious
teaching in any organized way, was forbidden.

This brief history of Romania highlights some
of the factors that are an integral part of the
ideological training today, especially in the areas
of nationalism and patriotism. An historical

perspective is necessary for a full understanding of many of the other political items in the ideology; the ideology of relations between nations as taught in the school can be easily understood in the context of Romania's history and the contemporary consciousness by Romanians of this history.

NOTES

1. Donald Catchlove, Romania's Ceausescu (Kent, England: Abacus Press, 1972), p. 21.

2. Field Notes, Kindergarten (Focal Unit of research), class period, February, 1972.

3. I asked more than twenty teachers from different schools the question quoted here. The answer is a summary of the replies. Field Notes, July, 1975.

4. Field Notes, February, 1972, same occasion as in no. 2.

5. Field Notes, Grade School, Grade IV (Focal Unit of research), October, 1972.

6. Field Notes, April 14, 1972 with the interviewee who is a member of the Romanian Academy. We spoke in French. I translate esprit as 'soul' in the second last line, taking esprit as a translation of the Romanian suflet, which means 'soul, spirit, mind'.

7. Georges Fotino, Contribution a l'etude des origines de l'ancien droit coutumier Roumain. Paris: L. Chauny et L. Quisnac, 1925.

   C. B. Dissesco, Les origines du droit Roumain. Paris: Typographie Chamerot et Renouard, 1889.

   R. W. Seton-Watson, A History of the Roumanians from Roman Times to the Completion of Unity. London: Cambridge University Press, 1934.

Matila C. Ghyka, A Documented Chronology of Roumanian History, trans. Fernand G. Renier and Anne Cliff. Oxford: B. H. Blackwell Ltd., 1941.

Ifor L. Evans, The Agrarian Revolution in Romania. London: Cambridge University Press, 1924.

8. Alexandru D. Xenopol, Istoria Romanilor din Dacia Trainana, Vol. I-III. Iasi: Saraga, 1896.

Nicolae Iorga, Histoire des Roumains de Transylvanie et de Hongrie, Vol. I,II. Bucharest: Joseph Gobl, 1915.

Miron Constantinescu et al., Istoria Romaniei. Bucuresti: Editura Didactica si Pedagogica, 1970.

Stephen Fischer-Galati, who is considered a world expert on Romania and an historian by profession, says in his Twentieth Century Romania (New York & London: Columbia University Press, 1970), p. 9, that "the Rumanians 'disappeared' from recorded history for nearly one thousand years." For a summary of an opposing viewpoint, see: Constantin C. Giurescu (ed.), Istoria Romaniei in Data. (Bucharest: Editura Enciclopedica Romana, 1971), pp. 41-56.

9. Eudokie Hurmuzaki in the last century was an historian who collected and published primary sources of historical documents. The Hurmuzaki series was added to by other Romanian historians, e.g., Nicolae Iorga, who contributed five volumes. see: William O. Oldson, The Historical and Nationalistic Thought of Nicolae Iorga (New York: Columbia University Press, 1973), p. 9.

10. Field Notes, July, 1974. Interviewee was not a faculty member of a Focal or Secondary Unit

High School.

11. Istoria Romaniei. Bucuresti: Editura de Stat,
    1947. Istoria R.P.R. Bucuresti: Editura
    Didactica si Pedagogica, 1952.

12. Field Notes, January 22, 1974. The inter-
    viewee is a specialist in the Philology of
    early Romanian.

13. Michael J. Rura, Reinterpretation of History
    as a Method of Furthering Communism in Ruma-
    nia. Washington, D.C.: Georgetown University
    Press, 1961.

14. This was explained to me as the section of the
    Communist Party that deals with 'agitation',
    and propaganda. The 'agitation' part was
    confined to the period before the C.P. comes
    to power. Field Notes, May, 1975.

15. Ghita Ionescu, Communism in Romania, 1944-62
    (London, New York & Toronto: Oxford Univer-
    sity Press, 1964), p. 179.

16. Iosif Chisinevschi, Leonte Rautu and Mihail
    Roller had been involved with Agitprop since
    the '30's; at various times they were direct-
    ors of Agitprop. Roller in particular was
    concerned with the ideological control of
    academicians and professors (see: ibid., p.
    45, 351, and 356). None of the three are
    ethnic-Romanians. Chisinevschi and Rautu
    spent the war years in Moscow and so belonged
    to the Muscovite group in the Romanian C. P.
    who were for the most part purged in the '50's
    and early '60's by the ethnic-Romanian faction
    in the C.P. of Romania. The text is from
    Field Notes, January 22, 1976, from the same
    interviewee as in no. 12. Four other profes-
    sors made similar comments.

17. Ion Ratiu, Contemporary Romania (Richmond,
    England: Foreign Affairs Publishing Co., Ltd.,
    1975), p. 53.

18. Field Notes, July, 1974. Interviewee was a faculty member at a High School in a Secondary Unit of research.

19. Ratiu, op. cit., p. 2.

20. This paragraph is a summary of more than twenty interviews. The same ideas were also told to me in many interviews with intellectuals who were not educators. Field Notes, March, 1976.

21. These Germans are the Sasi (The Saxons) as distinct from the other German group that live in the Banat region of Romania, the Schwabians. The Saxon dialect of German in Romania is sui generis, with many medieval usages and patterns. Saxons in Romania are traditionally Lutheran. The Szeklers are now Magyarized and belong in the main, to the Catholic religion; their origins are uncertain.

22. This is the prototype of the Western myth of the Dracula, but in Romania, Vlad is a hero-warrior who dealt severely with the Turks. See: Radu Florescu and Raymond T. Mc Nally, Dracula: a biography of Vlad the Impaler, 1431-1476. New York: Hawthorn Books Inc., 1973.

23. Avram Iancu is a popular folk-hero in Romania. He is called King of the Mountains in popular songs and poems (craiul Muntilor). This is significant in that Avram Iancu is portrayed as the modern hero who continues the Daco-Roman tradition of hiding out in the mountains from the enemy. Iancu was an attorney who adopted peasant dress and customs, so he is also portrayed as the intellectual who led the peasants by becoming at heart a peasant also.

24. Rura, op. cit., pp. 17-23.

25. Ibid., p. 36.

26. Gilberg Trond, Modernization in Romania since World War II (New York: Praeger, 1975), p. 85.

27. Field Notes, December, 1973. The interviewee is a sub-Director in an Institute of Higher Education.

28. London: Oxford University Press, 1964. The lengthy introduction covers the period up to 1944.

29. Rura, op. cit., documents the official version of Romanian history in the '50's. The present official version is now quite different from that in the '50's. What has not changed is the emphasis on class struggle and the general Marxist philosophy of historical evolution.

30. Field Notes, Grade VI in a Grade School, Secondary Unit of Research, February, 1973.

31. Ionescu, op. cit., p. 19.

32. It was only in the early '50's that the Romanization in the leadership of the Romanian Communist Party took place. The beginning of Romanization in the Romanian Communist Party is dated from the elections for office in the C.P. on March 13, 1951 (Ionescu, op. cit., p. 209). At this time also, anti-semitism was spreading throughout Eastern Europe; many of the leaders in the Romanian Communist Party were Jewish. It was in January of 1953 that the 'Jewish doctor' persecution started in the Soviet Union with Stalin personally supervising the torture and interrogation of the Jewish doctors. see: Isaac Deutscher, Stalin (London: Oxford University Press, 2nd ed., 1967), p. 620.

33. See: Ionescu, op. cit., pp. 5-28; Ratiu, op.

cit., p. 3.

34. Ian M. Matley, Romania (New York: Praeger, 1970), p. 113.

35. See: Bela Vago, The Shadow of the Swastika: the Rise of Fascism and anti-Semitism in the Danube Basin, 1936-1939 (Farnborough, Hants, England: Saxon House, 1975), pp. 19-73, for Romanian fascism. See, also, Ibid., p. 173, Diplomatic Document no. 6, for the report of Sir R. Hoare to Anthony Eden confirming the popularity of fascism among the student body in Romania during the pre-war period.

36. Field Notes, Focal Unit of research, May, 1975.

37. Ionescu, op. cit., p. 59.

38. Field Notes, October, 1974. Interviewee is a faculty member in a department outside the Focal and Secondary Units of research.

39. Ibid., p. 61.

40. Ibid., pp. 84-6.

41. Ratiu, op. cit., p. 3.

42. Sir Winston Churchill, The Second World War, vi, Triumph and Tragedy (London: Cassell, 1954), p. 198.

43. Deutscher, op. cit., p. 544.

44. This is a figure estimated from official sources; see: Ratiu, op. cit., p. 8, for discussion and evidence.

45. A copy of the official abdication that the King was compelled to sign is reproduced in Catchlove, op. cit., p. 99.

46. Ionescu, op. cit., p. 133.

47. Ghita Ionescu, The Reluctant Ally (London: Ampersand, 1965), p. 22.

48. Starvation and famine can remain as strong entities as 'myth' in the cultural memory of a people. The Irish famine of 1844, for example, is still an important cultural memory, because the starvation was caused politically when meat and grain was taken as tribute by the occupying power leaving only the blighted potato for the indigenous population. In Romania, the memory of the food being taken away from the country, causing starvation, becomes important in the study of communist training because of the common linking of Soviet control and the process of the country becoming communist.

49. For a detailed discussion of hasty recruitment and the condemnation of this by Gheorghiu-Dej, the leader of Romania until his death in 1965, see: Ionescu, Communism in Romania, 1944-1962, p. 119.

50. Scinteia, 12/7/1961. Quoted in Ibid., p. 201.

CHAPTER IV

IDEOLOGICAL TRAINING IN THE KINDERGARTEN
AND GRADE SCHOOL

I am taking the Kindergarten with the Grade
School, because much of the training in the Kin-
dergarten is the same or similar to the Grade
School especially in grades I-IV.

Part I: The Kindergarten

The research in the Focal Unit of the Kindergarten study serves as the main source for this
report. The observation and interviews in the
Secondary Units and the interviews with students
and faculty from other Kindergartens serve two
purposes. Firstly, what is included in the report
on the Focal Unit was also found in kind, in the
Secondary Units. A teacher in a Secondary Unit
may have used different choreography in a dance to
teach about the value and beauty of physical work
than a teacher in the Focal Unit, but the theme of
the dance in both instances is the same.[1] An item
found in the Focal Unit had to be found also in
the Secondary Units to be included in the report.
Secondly, I will use examples from the Secondary
Units and the interviews in the general category
to reinforce or clarify by example, what is found
in the Focal Unit.

I am not dividing ideology into political and
moral ideology. In Romania, acts such as the individual pursuit of pleasure and the use of con-
traceptives, for example, have a political interpretation. What may be categorized in some cultures as pertaining to purely personal morality,
motive for example, officially belongs in Romania
to social morality, and whatever is social, is political. Social behavior is the outcome of political organization. It would be erroneous to cate-
gorize an item, such as not telling lies in the
official ideological training as Personal Morality.
Because I am describing official Romanian training

in ideology, I use the only category used officially, the socio-political. Someone steals something at work; this is regarded officially in the
eyes of the law as political sabotage. If children in the Kindergarten are taught cleanliness or
the importance of being first, these items are
presented as socio-political acts. Society needs
clean teeth if it is going to have healthy workers. Romania wants to succeed. Work hard, come
first in the class. Romania needs her best to do
their best. Everything is moral, social, and political, at the same time. But moral and social
are aspects of the political. This applies not
only to overt and covert behavior, but also to
the quality of the action. A worker turns a
piece of metal on the lathe. This is a social
act; it benefits society. It is also political
because it benefits Romania, and the Party that
guides and rules Romania. The worker must do his
action for the official social and political motives. Not only must his motives be such, but he
must engage in the action with enthusiasm for the
country and the Party. So every action, and motivation for every action, must be done in conformity with official policy. The quality of the
action and the motivation can only be of the
quality deemed perfect by the Communist Party.

Section 1: Content of Ideology in the Kindergarten

The child in Romania before he or she goes to
Kindergarten calls all adults apart from parents,
'auntie' (tante) or 'uncle' (nene). The child
does not normally address adults as Mr., Mrs., or
Miss. All adults are, linguistically, part of the
extended family. The child goes to school; all
adults at schools are addressed as 'Comrade'
(Tovaris).

Because of the way the following three items
are presented in the training they can be classified together. These three items are the President, the Communist Party, and Romania. Classi-
fying the three items together is possible because
the analogies used for each form a unit.

96

Item	Analogy
The President	Father
The Party	Family
The Country	Home

A: The President

The President is presented as the Father of
all. In one story he is presented as the Father
who went to prison to free his children because
he loved them.[2] In another Kindergarten class the
President is presented in a poem as "The Father
who feeds his children, loves his children."[3] In
the same period the teacher pointed to pictures on
the wall. In the photographs the President was
surrounded by children, receiving flowers from a
child, kissing a child. The same teacher said
every Romanian has two fathers: 'father at home
and our Father, Nicolae Ceausescu'. When I asked
four children in the Kindergarten after the class
at playtime: "Who is your father?", two answered
Nicolae Ceausescu, one said he did not know and
the fourth said: "Big Father and Small Father".[4]

When I asked a Kindergarten teacher whether
the children were confused with being told the
President was their father, she recited the version of the prayer: "Our Father". "Our Father who
art in the palace, hallowed be thy name, thine is
the kingdom, thy will be done in heaven as it is
on earth . . . ."[5]

In the Kindergarten the President is presented as 'a hero and the first son of the Romanian
people', 'Nicolae the Great', 'the ray of the
sun',[6] and other such phrases of compliment, and
direct historical comparisons such as 'the new
Decebal'.[7]

The President is also presented with his official titles, principally, "President of the Socialist Republic of Romania", and "Secretary General of

the Romanian Communist Party".

A Kindergarten teacher from a secondary unit of research said in an interview[8] that the Party Secretary in the school had given instructions that each week one or more periods should be devoted to telling the children the weekly news. This would involve frequently telling the children of the speeches and actions of the President: his visits to factories and to the countryside, his visits abroad; his speeches during Party gatherings and visits to various institutions and places in the countryside.

Indirect training also takes pleace. Each child has a little flag of Romania. At school gatherings and demonstrations the children sometimes waved their flags and chanted 'Ceausescu, P.C.R.'. This was also observed in the classroom. There was a poem celebrating the President. After the poem the teacher had all the children rise and chant, 'Ceausescu, P.C.R.'.[9]

In each Kindergarten where I did research, there was a large picture of the President in the entrance hall. There was also at least one picture in each classroom, sometimes numerous photographs of the President in the presence of little children, kissing them or receiving flowers from them.

The name of the President was used to teach the five year olds the alphabet and the formation of words.[10] During December of 1972, in the secondary unit of research, the children were preparing an art piece as a present for the President's birthday. The teacher in the same class told me that was the custom in many schools.[11]

The President was also included in other aspects of the ideology as the authoritative source. For example, in a lesson about the importance of work, the lesson was prefaced by "Our beloved President has told us . . . ."[12] In another Kindergarten class when the teacher was explaining to the

98

children how each person must work hard for the
building up of Romania she said during the lesson:
"The President loves the children who work hard,
the best."[13]

I asked each of the five teachers whom I interviewed in the Focal Unit, the question: "What
are the ideas that you have to teach in the Kindergarten?" Each of the answers included the
President and the Party.

B: The Party

"What is the Party? The Party is the big
family of all Romanians who love the country of
Romania."[14] The analogy of the family was used on
many occasions for the Party during the observations in the Kindergarten. When I asked a group
of five four-year-old children in the Focal Unit,
what the Party was, they did not know. Of six
five-year-olds, two did not know and four answered
'the communists'.[15]

When I asked the teachers whether the idea of
family was also used in the Kindergarten to apply
to the children, they answered no. They seemed
perplexed at the question, as if they did not com-
prehend the implications of the question. I asked
whether the teacher and the children in a room
were a commune or a group. The answers in general
were, 'Yes, a group, a class'. There was frequent
group activity observed in the various Kindergartens but the reason behind the group activity
seemed to be pragmatic. If there was one teacher
and 20-30 children, there had to be group activity.
But I could find no evidence of a philosophy fostering a group or family consciousness among the
children or faculty. Individual expression and
individual striving to be first are encouraged in
the Romanian Kindergarten in all activities. The
best in the class were praised and selected as examples; some were given awards, materially or by
position in class or in line.

The notion of family then is confined to the

99

Party. The biological family is also given stress in the Kindergarten. I asked ten children including both four and five-year-olds, from the three units of research: "Who is your family?"[16] The answer always included biological parents, but never the Party.

There were many references to the Communist Party in prose lessons, in the words of songs, in poems, in declarations, such as 'Long Live the Romanian Communist Party'. The Party was referred to in the following ways: 'the savior of the country', 'the only Party', 'the Party which supplies all our needs', 'the Party which we love', 'the Party which loves us', 'the spiritual life'.

There were stories that teachers told their children that had as their theme the persecution of the Party by the fascists in Romania and the Nazis; the heroism of the Party in dying and suffering for the workers and peasants; the love the Party has for peace; the love the Party has for children. The children, before the Party came were hungry, had to work, and did not have a chance to go to school.

Stories were told about how children helped the Party in the illegalist period before 1944. The children were put in jail by the evil men. There were also stories of heroism from the post-1944 period, stories of sacrifices that children made for the Party.

The terms 'Party' and 'Communists' are freely interchanged. I never heard the phrase 'member of the Party', in the Kindergarten.

There was some indirect training in the drawing period and the writing period. For example, the children in preparation for the Party Congress, were drawing people working. The letters P.C.R. (Romanian Communist Party), were written in sequence during the teaching and learning of the alphabet. In writing class children were learning to write the words, 'Partidul Communist Roman'.

C: The Country

The term sometimes used in the analogy for
Romania was casa noastra (lit. 'our house', or
'home'). The ideological training with regard to
Romania had a double thrust. There was the historical perspective which included both nationalism and patriotism; and a purely affective perspective which involved only patriotism.

The historical perspective followed the pattern outlined in Chapter III. In general, in the
Kindergarten, in the historical perspective, the
stress was more on patriotism than on nationalism.
Nationalism was only introduced when for example,
the courage of Romanian heroes was explained: that
they fought and died defending Romania against the
enemy.

In the Kindergarten the teachers told the
children about Romania's ethnic origins. That Romanians were Daco-Romans, a mixture of the Dacians
and the Romans. That Romanian is a Latin language.

In one class there was a dramatization, played by the children, of a meeting between the Dacians led by Decebal and the Romans. The meeting
was peaceful, with each of the two groups greeting
and praising the other. Decebal says: "Our two
people will be the beginning of a great people,[17]
the Romanians."

The names of the Romanian heroes who defended
Romania against her enemies and fought for independence are of two kinds. They include the traditional heroes such as Mihai and Stephen. But
only Romanian communists are included for the period of the last hundred years. In the Kindergarten, I never heard mention of the role of the
Soviet Union after World War II. A Director of a
Kindergarten in the Secondary Unit of research explained the omission of the Soviet Union by say-[18]
ing: 'We are our own bosses now'.

The Directors of the Kindergarten institutions

in each sector in Bucharest meet once a month with officials from the Ministry of Education. At these meetings the general plan of what should be taught is given. The Director mentioned above told me in the same interview that the Soviet Union was not being omitted, but the Romanian role was sufficient because of the children's limited development.

The historical perspective pervades much of the patriotic training at least by allusion. But there is also training in patriotism on a purely affective level. The stories and poems about Romania resemble love poems.

'My country with eyes so beautiful'.
'Romania, our land, rich in flowers'.
'Romania, Romania, home of our ancestors'.
'Your mountains and lakes
Your rivers and streams
I love you for your beauty'.[19]

Romania is praised for her richness and bounty. Romania is the country where everything is done for the sake of the children; the children in turn are exhorted to work hard because of love for Romania. Romania is praised for her music, her painting, her sculpture, her literature.

The children in turn learn by heart and recite stories and poems, and sing songs in praise of Romania. Words and short sentences in praise of Romania are used by the five year olds in the writing class.

The total appeal to the emotions in the training in patriotism is intentional, as being suited to the conceptual maturation level of four-to-five year olds. One young Kindergarten teacher explained their training as Kindergarten teachers in the Pedagogical Institute as emphasizing: the emotional foundation of attachment and enthusiasm must be built up when the children are very young, to serve as the basis for the intellectual adherence later in life.[20]

I have presented the training with regard to
the President, the Party, and Romania separately.
But the three often are presented as a unit.
Nicolae Ceausescu is the President of Romania, a
Communist, the leader of the Party. Everything he
says and does is for Romania. The Party is the
true spirit of Romania.

D: Work, Success, Discipline

The next item that I am going to deal with is
'work' and 'success'. It is important for every
true Romanian to strive for success, because the
children are the communists of the future. The
unitary trust in promoting patriotism, communism,
hard work, and success is the President's own
philosophy of Romanian communism.

'Work' or 'labor' is one of the key concepts
in Marxism. 'Work' is sometimes presented as an
end in itself; sometimes it is presented as a
means.[21] Work is presented in an abstract, almost
mystical way, as something which has its own existence, its own reason, its own beauty. But work
is usually presented to the children as necessary
if they are going to be successful. I never heard
during the observations on any school level, reference to collective work. Only, 'you the individual, must work hard if you are going to be
successful'. Individual children are praised constantly for their answers. Teachers would say to
me in a loud voice for all the children to hear,
that a particular child was the best in the class
at art, writing, singing, reciting, dancing, acting. Individual pieces of work were often on the
walls with 1, 2, 3 on them and the names of the
children. When I asked a group of Kindergarten
teachers about the fostering of work, competition
and individual rewarding in the Kindergarten, they
laughed at me.[22] They asked me why Romania should
be different from other societies. The parents
want their children to be successful; the Director
wants the children in her school to be better than
those in other schools; the teacher is blamed if
some children are poor achievers. One teacher in

the group put the matter rather bluntly to me.
'If you had not been a success in school you
would be a manual worker now or a Kindergarten
teacher.' The image of me as a Kindergarten
teacher was funny to them.

Even in 1973 I was still operating with an
assumption of what communism should be. The sin-
gling out of individuals for praise and prizes,
because they were the best, did not seem to be in
accord with my conception of communism. But in
pursuing the question of the advocation of success,
perhaps for the wrong reasons, I realized over a
number of years the importance of 'success' in the
ideological training. Children in the Kindergarten are given homework, both artistic and academic. Some children are provided with private tuition, paid for by their parents, outside the
school system.

Upward mobility within the structure, K-University, depends on success. But the teachers in
the Kindergarten directly teach the value of success and the value of work in leading to success.
The training is done by exhortation. Obedience
and discipline are also linked to success. Obedience in practice means doing what the teachers
want a child to do. This also involves being po-
lite to the teacher and always calling her 'comrade'. The child in general is reprimanded for
initiating behavior of any kind. Obedience to
discipline, and politeness become factors in the
assessment of the child's success. Throughout the
Romanian school system, and starting with Kindergarten, children are given a grade on their reaction to discipline. This is included in the individual's scholastic record which is made available to teachers.

Obedience and politeness is directly advocated
within the Kindergarten. There is also indirect
training in discipline. There are rewards and
sanctions. Obedience to discipline is praised and
graded; failure is punished in various ways. Punishment can be a verbal reprimand, a poor grade, a

104

letter to parents, a visit to the Director or physical punishment such as isolation from the group activity. Corporal punishment is forbidden in Romanian schools.

Obedience at home is also advocated in the Kindergarten. The mother receives special mention as the target of love. There are poems used in the Kindergarten about the love of a mother, the love of a child for a mother.

'The name, the most beautiful of all words, Mother'. Teachers when they wished to improve a child sometimes made reference to: 'what would Mama say if she saw this?' I never heard mention of the Father of the children, in this context.

Items also found in the Kindergarten, in both direct and indirect training, are the following:[23] exhortations to be good, to be serious, to be honest, conscientious, not to steal, not to lie, to help the teacher.

In the Kindergarten there is little practical training in work. Sometimes the children are told that they must keep their country clean and beautiful by picking up papers inside and outside the school. This kind of work is sometimes extended to a nearby playground or park, and is called patriotic work.

On the Kindergarten level, I never observed any negative ideological training attacking, for example, other systems such as imperialism, capitalism, or colonialism.

Section 2: The Mode of the Ideological Training in the Kindergarten

The modes of training can be generally classified as (a) direct and verbal and, (b) indirect.

The teacher directly teaches items in the ideology using verbal exhortation, stories, songs, and poems. The children write the items as they

learn to write. The children also learn short
stories, songs, and poems by heart which incorporate ideological items. The children recite in
group or singly.

The teacher indirectly trains the students in
ideology by reward and punishment. The teacher
and the children engage in dance that incorporates
ideological items. Thematic dance, for example,
is used to train the children in the ideological
value of work. Sometimes verbalization is used in
the dance but usually the dance uses only movement
and gesture and non-verbal sounds. For example,
stylized movements are used to convey the actions
of a furnace worker, turning the body, pulling
with the arms. The peasant sows the seeds, walking and scattering with the fingers. The builder
hammers, saws, lays the bricks.

There is also indirect training by the use of
art. Aspects of Romania are drawn by the children. Workers of various kinds are drawn. Art
pieces are drawn as presents for the President.

Dramatization is a combination of movement
and language but is performed by the students as
directed by the teacher. Drama is used extensively
to teach the different epochs in Romanian history
that are officially important today. In brief
these are, (a) Romania's origins, (b) The traditional heroes up to the 19th century, (c) the
saving of Romania by the Communists, (d) incidents
in the life of President Nicolae Ceausescu.

Part II: The Grade School
Section 1: Grades I-IV

Over 90% of the students in the Grade School
which functioned as the Focal Unit of research had
spent at least one year in Kindergarten. They had
already mastered the fundamentals of reading and
writing; they could read simple text and write
certain words and phrases.

In the first four grades the primary emphasis

in the curriculum is on reading, writing, and arithmetic. Art, singing, and physical education together make up a quarter of the curriculum.

The main differences in the ideological training between Kindergarten and Grades I-IV are the following. The training is more direct and verbal in Grades I-IV than in the Kindergarten, as the competence in reading and writing continues. The children, as homework, learn by heart stories, poems, and songs containing ideological items. The children have to read as homework, children's magazines such as Arici-pogonici and Luminita which contain a digest of weekly political and economic news, as well as general items and items dealing with ideology. As the writing of the children improves, the children write stories, essays, and poems as homework; the topics are frequently ideological, dealing in the main with some aspect of Romania.

Ideology becomes now something that the young student gradually learns like any other subject; the teacher asks questions about ideology, the student must know the answers. The student learns the answers by heart, at home during homework, or writes the answers to ideological questions, in the catechism form of question and answer, or in essay form.

Singing and dance remain on the curriculum, but only for two hours a week. There is a corresponding lessening of ideological training using singing and dancing as the mode of training in Grades I-IV, as compared to the Kindergarten where singing and dancing are given twelve hours a week.

The ideological training in Grades I-IV becomes more direct, more verbal, more ideational than in the Kindergarten. The training is similar however in the Kindergarten and Grades I-IV in content. There is a slight increase in patriotic work but the patriotic work remains as in the Kindergarten, cleaning in and around the school, or in the vicinity of the school.

107

The ideological training remains affective, with the continuing stress on affection for the President, the Party, and Romania. The training continues to be positive. In Grades I-IV, I found no evidence of negative training which would involve, for example, a condemnation of factors not acceptable to the official ideology.

An important difference between Kindergarten and Grades I-IV is the increasing role relationship of the students with the ideological training. In Grades I-IV, the ideological training starts to resemble academic subjects where the students have increasing obligations towards the ideological training. They study factors about the Party and the country in school; they write about these factors in school and in their homework. They are tested in school on their knowledge of ideology. The training in Grades I-IV, while remaining affective, also becomes formalized on the basis of role obligations.

I kept close contact with two students through Grades III and IV in 1974 and 1975. Topics for essays to be done for homework included: 'The Communist Party is the only Party of Romanians'; 'The Party is the Party of all Workers'; 'Romania loves Peace'; 'The Importance of the Five Year Plan'.[24] Parental help is needed by the students in writing these essays. The parents of the children are urged at PTA meetings to help their children with homework. Thus, the parents of the students in Grades I-IV became involved in the ideological training in the schools indirectly. The essays containing ideology are graded as part of the homework in the writing classes, so that ideology and writing became a unit. In Grades I-IV, reading and writing constitute half of the curriculum in Grade I, and a third by Grade IV. Teachers maintain that the children are not capable of writing their essays at home without help; parents then, if concerned about their children's grades, must help with the essays which also contain ideological themes.

Section 2: Grades V-VIII

The ideological training in Grades V-VIII assumes a formalized framework through an organization called the Pioneers, as well as the training during the school day.

A: The Pioneers

The organization of the Pioneers was founded in 1949 after the model of the Pioneers in the Soviet Union. It was part of the Union of Communist Youth, making it directly a part of the Communist Party management. The children took a solemn oath of allegiance on the Romanian flag; the oath was similar to that taken by Soviet students.

In 1966, the beginning of the Ceausescu era, there took place a restructuring of the Pioneers. The Pioneers came under the Ministry of Education, with the Assistant Minister of Education becoming the head of the Pioneers. Before 1966, teachers in the schools were not responsible for the organization and management of the Pioneers on the school level. But in 1966, when the Pioneers' management came under the control of the Ministry of Education, teachers in the schools became the organizers of the Pioneers. Officially it is said that responsibility for the Pioneers was taken from the special instructors for the Pioneers and given to the teachers because, (a) the work of the teachers often ran parallel with the work of the instructors and, (b) "Too great an amount of work lay heavy on the young instructors' shoulders, while a considerable reserve of educational factors remained unused."[25] Unofficially, I was told that teachers now have responsibility for the Pioneers for two reasons. It saves money to have teachers do the work because teachers get no extra pay for the extra-school work with the Pioneers. Attendance at Pioneers events outside of school time is obligatory for teachers and students.[26] Secondly, teachers under the new system become directly responsible for all of the training of the children; teachers who are not members of the Communist Party

109

become agents of the Party in the training of the children outside of school.

In the Grade School, each teacher who does not have heavy administrative duties, is a 'commander' of a group of Pioneers. The groups form a 'detachment'. Three 'detachments' become a 'unit'. The military analogy is also used in designating members. Students are Pioneers and 'front' Pioneers if they have received high grades for a period of three years in school. In Romania, all levels of education evaluation is on a scale of 1-10. To become a 'front' Pioneer, a student must receive a score of 9 or 10 over a three year period. A detachment composed of 'front' Pioneers becomes a 'front' detachment. In the official explanation, distinctions and awards are the "conscious institutionalization of success"; success acts as an obligation, it is a duty of the successful subject to the collectivity which grants him the success."[27]

The Pioneers wear red scarves around the neck and berets with a Pioneer badge. The regulations of the Pioneers and oath of induction after 1966, "omit all reference to the 'great Soviet Union' and its youth organization and place greater emphasis on the education of Pioneers on the spirit of 'socialist patriotism' and love for the 'Romanian people, the Socialist Republic of Romania, and the Romanian Communist Party'."[28] Pioneers practice drill and, when outside the classroom, walk in double file.

The Pioneers organization has two functions. It supplements and complements education. Some of the activity of the Pioneers, compliments the academic education of the schools by giving the children an opportunity to play games, engage in hobbies, and enjoy the outdoors. The Pioneers also supplements the normal educational system by increasing the time given to academic and ideological training outside the normal class period.

Groups of students under a teacher as commander, spend one period a week within the school, but outside school hours, in direct ideological training. This involves for example training in political structures and civics in general; the purpose is that the young Pioneers acquire civic qualities.[29] The students of Grade VI in the Grade School which served as the Focal Unit of research, for example, in 1974, learned about the organization of the People's Council in their district of Bucharest; this included the mode of election and the mode of appointment of candidates for election; the names of the various committees of the People's Council and their functions. In the same year, Grade VII was beginning to study national State structure. The Secondary Units of research on the Grade School level, had similar programs as the Focal Unit in civics. There are competitions for choosing the best students in civics in the class, school, district, county, and national levels.

During the school year, on weekends and also during vacations, the teacher-commanders of the Pioneers take their groups on visits to the Party Museum and the Museum of History, where the teachers and museum personnel give talks on aspects of the history of the Party and Romania. The students are also given a guided tour of selected exhibits in the museums.

The visits to the Museum of History over a four year period go through the periods and events outlined in Chapter III, with a special emphasis on Romania's traditional heroes. One particular hero is chosen as the personage for the day. Modern history is also included. In the modern period mention is made of the Royal Family, but in a negative way. But teachers told me in interviews that the negativism officially accorded the role of the Royal Family in Romania's history, is more like praise if compared to the more extreme negativism of the '50's and early '60's. In the period 1971-'76, praise was given to some Romanians of this century who were not Communists, such as Nicolae Iorga, the historian.

In visits to the Party Museum, stress is given to the heroic fight of the Party, especially in the illegalist period before 1944, when the Communist Party was banned in Romania. Youths who were members of the Party who died in battle, or were killed by Government forces, or by the Iron Guard, are given special prominence. The primary focus in the Party Museum is given to the youth, the imprisonment and general life story of Nicolae Ceausescu. All students during their V-VIII school years visit at least once, the Doftana prison and the other prisons where Nicolae Ceausescu was imprisoned with other Party members and political prisoners. Doftana prison is now a major National monument.

In the Party museum, the format of the visit is similar to a visit to the Museum of History; a lecture on a particular topic and a visit to selected aspects of the Museum's display. In 1975, there were at least six visits to the Party Museum and five visits to the Museum of History by the students in Grades V-VIII in the Focal Unit. As homework, students write an account of the visit to the Museum, which includes the particular theme of the visit, such as the strike of the railway workers at Grivita.

During vacation periods, teachers take their Pioneers to films and plays that have ideological themes. The themes may be historical and patriotic, such as the different films dealing with aspects of the life of Michael the Brave. The themes may be items from the official history of the Party, or items of contemporary ideological importance, such as heroism among the workers of a construction company, or the ship building industry. Most plays and films of contemporary ideological importance have the following format; corrupt management exposed by Junior management or workers who are Communist Party activists.

Although the administration of the Pioneers is within the Ministry of Education and the elementary school system in general, there is also a supervisory body, the National Council of the Pioneers' Organization which is an organ of the Central Committee of the Communist Party. President Nicolae Ceausescu's brief to the National Council of the Pioneers was "to spare no effort so that those who carry on the work of building Socialism and Communism on the soil of our Country shall live up to the grand task assigned them by history, to ensure the permanent progress of our homeland, the welfare of the Romanian people."[30] The National Council of the Pioneers checks on whether the regular activities of a Pioneer group contain ideological input.

The Pioneers organization belongs officially to the category of front organizations. Front organizations function as the means by which all members of the society are mobilized by the Communist Party. In this way people who are not members of the Communist Party are linked to the teachings and directives of the Party on a continual basis.

Mobilization also involves attendance at demonstrations. Teachers take their Pioneers in individual groups, or all the teachers in a school take all the Pioneers in the school, to demonstrations. Demonstrations are of different kinds. In the academic year, 1974-'76, the students from Grades V-VII in the Focal Unit of research, went to the following kinds of demonstrations. They went at various times to a position along the route on the way from the airport, as a line of honor when the President escorted a leader from another country. They attended Party rallies in the Palace square. They attended a ceremony in honor of Dimitrie Cantemir, the hero-scholar of the century. They attended and participated in ceremonies for National Day, May 1st and the annual Festival of Sport.

Attendance at demonstrations involves a minimum of four hours in standing position or marching formation. Sometimes the Pioneers participated by dancing the traditional Romanian dance, the Hora

113

Unirii (The Dance of Unity), by singing patriotic
songs, by chanting Ceausescu, P.C.R. Sometimes
demonstrations are confined to the school, honor-
ing a Romanian hero or a Party event such as the
President's birthday.

The Pioneers in class, school, district, municipality or national groupings participate in
cultural events. There are concerts and social
evenings with patriotic and Party themes. In
school events, students recite poetry, enact short
dramas, sing, and dance. Some of the lyric poetry
is composed by the students. There are competitions yearly in Romania for students and non-stu-
dents in composing poetry containing patriotic and
Party themes. The competitions are on every level, from the class to the national level. The
winning poems of the competitions on every level
serve as the source material for the cultural
events featuring patriotic and Party themes. The
cultural events attended by the Pioneers may be
sponsored by the school, the district, the municipality, or the nation as a whole.

Every Pioneer participates in the competitions
which begin on the Grade level, of writing poetry
and prose containing patriotic and Party themes.
Students recite their own poetry on the grade level. Winners recite their works on the levels
where they win the competitions, except on the
national level which is presented on television.

On the grade level, students write a minimum
of four pieces. The student recites his or her
own poetry by heart. Students also learn by heart
published patriotic or Party poetry and the lyrics
of patriotic songs. Individuals and the group sing
the patriotic songs. The dances at the cultural
events reflect Party themes of work and unity; or
patriotic themes reflecting episodes from Romanian
folklore and history, such as weaving, mowing by
scythe, or a victory by the folk-hero, Avram Iancu.

The last aspect of the Pioneers' activity involving ideological training is the organized ex-

cursion. The excursion may be for a few hours, one day, a weekend, or weeks in the summer. Excursions are to factories, farms, and places of historical and Party interest in the city and in the countryside. Excursions are compulsory except for the excursions to summer camp, which are over a period of weeks in the summer. The excursion to a particular factory or farm takes place usually during the winter and spring vacations. On one visit to a factory in 1974,[31] the teacher-commander of the Pioneer group told me the format of a visit to a factory or farm.

(a) Short talk in school on the importance of the economy in the development of Socialism and Communism.

(b) Brief description of the type of work done in the place to be visited.

(c) Tour of the place of work, with a descriptive talk by a Party activist of the factory or farm.

During excursions of the duration of a weekend or longer, cultural events are included with a recitation of patriotic and Party poetry and the singing of patriotic and Party songs. A day in the summer camp or during a weekend excursion begins with a talk by the teacher-commander of the Pioneer group, dealing with an aspect of Socialist morality such as obedience, honesty, and zeal in promoting the Party cause because of love of the country.

Through the Pioneers organization, the student at the age of ten, is first introduced into the ideological mobilization of the adult world. The role aspects of the ideological training are increased by the compulsory attendance at Party and State demonstrations and cultural events which have patriotic and Party themes. The student increasingly takes on obligations towards the ideology, such as writing poetry with ideological themes. The affective-type language in the ideo-

115

logical training is similar to that used in the
Kindergarten with respect to the President, the
Party, and the country. But with the introduction
of concepts such as the economy, the ideological
training through the Pioneers has reached an
ideational level different from the almost purely
sentimental level of the ideological training in
the Kindergarten and Grades I-IV.

B: Grades V-VIII

While dealing with the Kindergarten, I mentioned that some students have private tutors who
are paid by students' parents. The Practice of
private tuition continues in Grades I-IV, but in-
creases in Grades V-VIII. Of one hundred freshmen
in a university department in September 1974, 90%
had private tuition for eight years before entering the university, which would include the period
when they were in Grades V-VIII.[32]   I could not
obtain exact figures for the private tuition in
Grades V-VIII, in any of the units of research.
But the teachers in these grades said that students
were already planning their personal specialization for High School. This involved a concentration in certain subjects, so that the last four
years of Grade School and the four years of High
School would be devoted particularly to the subjects which would appear in the entrance examination in the department of the University of the
student's choice.

The entrance examination for every University
department involves a section on ideology. While
the teachers in Grades V-VIII could not give exact
figures for the numbers of students in their
classes who take private tuition in ideology, they
estimated the number as everyone whose grades are
poor, who want to go to University. A poor grade
is 8/10 or under.

Students in Grades V-VIII who want to enter
an academic-type High School which has a high track
record for University entrants, must have a 9/10
or 10/10 score from Grades V-VIII.

The academically oriented ideological training in Grades V-VIII resembles the usual academic
subject with instruction, reading, homework, testing, and grading. Each class on each grade level,
in grades V-VIII, has a home-room teacher who is
responsible for the discipline and correct ideological behavior of the students. The student in
Grade V is already a teenager.

Appearance is part of correct ideological behavior. All students wear school uniforms. Girls
wear their hair short or tied back; boys have
short back and sides. Boys wear short trousers.
The Director of the school periodically checks the
dress, hair-style, and general appearance of students at the school gate. But it is the direct
responsibility of the home-room teacher to check
daily the appearance of the students.

In Grades V-VIII negativism is introduced into the ideological training. Anything contrary to
official ideology is negative. Failure to obey
the dress code is ideologically incorrect behavior,
or decadent. Teachers in Grades V-VIII said that
there was trouble only with the working-class and
the 'gypsies', who were not directed properly at
home. The freshmen whom I interviewed in 1974 a-
bout their private tuition, said that in general
they conformed with the codes of public behavior
in Grades V-VIII.

The students in Grades V-VIII obtain their
ideological training through three main sources:
(a) from their home-room teacher, (b) the history
class, and (c) in the literature class.

(a) The home-room teacher has three functions. She is the administration's contact with
the students, the counselor to the students, and
the ideological instructor. The last two functions
are both supervisory and instructional with regard
to ideology. The following is an example of negative supervision. A student in Grade VII told the
history teacher the Russians had made a treaty
with the Nazis in the beginning of the war which

had been the reason Romania had not joined the allies in World War II. The student was sent to the home-room teacher, whom I interviewed during the same month.³³ I had been interviewing in the fall of 1974, studying how the students learn what not to say. In the training I had been observing the official ideology, and had observed few instances of negativism in the replies of students.

The home-room teacher told me she talked to the parents of the student explaining how their child's behavior could lead to visitation of the school by the district inspectorate and probably a check of the whole school by the Ministry of Education and the Central Committee of the Party. Every person in Romania over the grade school age knew about the Russian pact with Hitler and the student was not incorrect, the home-room teacher said. But the history teacher, the home-room teacher, the Party Secretary, the Party Committee in the school, the Director of the school and the school district would be under investigation if the one instance was not confined to the one instance. The student was kept at home for a week by his parents in an unofficial suspension by the school. The home-room teacher had told the parents that one other such instance could jeopardize the student's chance of going to a University. The Party Committee had probably entered the incorrect behavior in the student's dossier, which was no longer with the rest of the students' files.

In general, teachers in the interviews said students learn what not to say from a multiple source. Teachers stay away from sensitive areas as much as possible. If discussion is allowed, then it must be guided in a closed fashion to allow only acceptable answers. If a 'smell' of incorrect behavior appears, the teacher reacts strongly against it, giving extra homework, for example, as punishment to show the teacher's displeasure. The teacher can always use the threat of poor grades which immediately gets the students in trouble with their parents. Peer competition for grades introduces the possibility of peer policing. As the students mature conceptually, the parents tell them the ideological facts of life; what can be said and what cannot be said unless the student does not care about his or her future, or the jobs of parents.

When I asked senior University students who were going to become teachers how they learned in Grade School what not to say, they said that peer influence and parental instruction were the important factors.[34] You hear something from your peers and tell your parents. The University students said that by Grade V or VI, students have learned the difference between positive and negative, public and private, official and unofficial and how to combine, for example, only the positive, public and official as behavioral response for the classroom situation.

The home-room teacher mentioned above also said that she uses the class-leader as the means of informing students. The class-leader is chosen because of high grades and political activism. Political activism in Grades V-VIII means that the student figures prominently as a leader at cultural events featuring patriotic and Party themes; gives the speeches at demonstrations and is highly active in the Pioneers.

In the case cited above, the home-room teacher told the class-leader that students should not talk about the Russians and the Nazis. The home-room teacher would not say this to the whole class publicly; the student could tell the class more discreetly. The home-room teacher also used the class-leader to reprimand or warn a group, or to convey information to the students if the information is about an event taking place before a class meeting with the home-room teacher.

In Grades V-VIII, the home-room teacher instructs the students in ideology. The curriculum in general for Grades V-VIII, is designed to keep the students informed of current events. Teachers use the Party newspaper Scinteia and the Party paper for the youth, Scinteia Tineretului, as source material. The home-room teacher at the Communist Party meeting of the school cell, or at the Union of Teachers meeting, receives a briefing from the Party Secretary of the school on what is to be stressed for the week. The home-room teachers that I interviewed and observed, read articles from one of the two newspapers. Teachers read the official newspaper for two reasons. Reading the newspaper is convenient, requiring little preparation; and you can never make an ideological mistake, if you read the official newspaper.

In general, whatever is given prominence in the newspaper is read by the home-room teacher in the period for ideology. The home-room teacher meets with the students at least once a week. In the Focal Unit and two of the Secondary Units, class with the home-room teacher was once a week, but more often at times of intense political activity such as plenary meetings of the Central Committees, election times, meetings of the Party Congress, the State Council, the Grand National Assembly and times of major speeches by the President. In four of the Grade Schools of the Secondary Unit of research, the home-room teacher had classes twice or three times a week with the students.

Topics in classes included: the speeches of the President; decrees of the Central Committee; the role of industry in the building of Communism in Romania; the importance of fulfilling the Five Year Plan in under five years.

As homework, students write essays on topics covered by the home-room teacher, or on topics to be researched in the newspapers by the students themselves, such as 'Romania and African States'. The student's essays are summaries of official policy. Just as in Grades I-IV, the essays on ideology can normally be done by the students only with adult or parental help. Some parents hire private tutors to help their children.

(b) Ideological training also takes place in the history class. For the four years from Grades V-VIII, students have two hours of history a week. The first three years cover ancient history, feudal times, and modern history on a global scale; in Grade VIII Romanian history is studied.

The Marxist model of Feudalism-Capitalism-Socialism is used in the analysis of global history with the stress, firstly, on the exploitation of the workers and peasants as slaves and serfs by the princes, and secondly on class warfare in the Capitalist stage. In Romanian history, two different models are used. The Marxist model explains the exploitation of the workers by the capitalist owners who were under, largely, non-Romanian influence. But a nationalist model is used in describing the Romanian heroes. The majority of the Romanian heroes were feudal lords, landlords, and capitalists, but the nationalist model focuses only on the heroic fight against the invaders of Romania, not on the heroes' aristocratic occupations and treatment of their serfs, peasants, and workers. In the context of Romanian history the nationalist model dominates over the Marxist model; a partial exception to this is the period 1944-1960, the period of the Soviet occupation and the first phase of communism. In general, there has been a rehabilitation of even avowed fascists who were nationalists. Some of the nationalist behavior of the Royal Family is acknowledged. Only the anti-communist nationalists of the post-1944 period have not been rehabilitated. The communist nationalists such as Patrascanu who were purged in 1944-1954 for their nationalism have, for the most part, been rehabilitated.

In the VIII Grade, the period of Romanian history in the years 1944-1955 is not given detailed treatment. The following items only are stressed:

(1) The Romanian army fought heroically at home and abroad against Fascism at the end of World War II.

121

(2) The Communist Party was democratically chosen by the people to form a Socialist Government.

(3) Capitalism was destroyed. Ownership and control passed to the dictatorship of the proletariat.

The educational and economic progress of Romania since the advent of communism forms the main thematic center of the study of contemporary Romanian history. The progress of Romania under communism is studied in greater detail in High School.

(c) In Grades V-VIII, the ideological concentration in the study of Romanian language and literature is on patriotism. Traditional pre-Communist, Romanian literature makes up the curriculum. The three primary ideological ideas are:

(1) The beauty of the Romanian language.

(2) The traditional Romanian themes expressing Romanian folk-culture.

(3) Patriotic themes.

The Romanian language expresses the creative suflet (mind, soul, spirit) of the Romanian neam (the nation, the ethnic people of the same ancestors, the family). The Romanian language expresses the Romanian dor (love, longing, desire). The students are told that the idea of dor can only be expressed in Romanian; and so cannot be translated. It expresses the Romanian's love and longing for his language, his family, his people, his country. Only the Romanian feels dor, and only the Romanian language can express the special bond between a patriot and his land and culture. The beauty of the Romanian language is also taught to the students in a pragmatic way, by the oral recitation of poetry and learning poetry by heart.

The use of Romanian as a literary language

only goes back to the last century. In Grades V-VIII, students read the novelists and poets from before 1939, especially works with themes from Romanian peasant life and folk-culture. These works give sociological and anthropological information about the way Romanians used to live. Many of the writers of folkloric themes are also used for their patriotic themes. The purpose of the readings in V-VIII is that students will imbibe today what a Romanian used to be, thus guaranteeing the diachronic unity of the people. The students read selections from writers such as Alexandrescu, Alexandri, Kogalniceanu, Negruzzi, and Filimon.

In Grades V-VIII, there is also indirect training through physical work. As in K-IV, the work is patriotic work but of a heavier variety. The students clear ground for planting; they plant trees and help adults in their voluntary or normal work.

In Grades V-VIII, the students are expected to play a bigger role in the reaction to the ideological training than students in K-IV. The role of the students has also been made organizational through induction into the Pioneers' organization. All the students in Grades V-VIII, in all the units of research were Pioneers. Students could not choose to opt out of the Pioneers.

In Grades V-VIII, the students were introduced to ideas and practices which are contrary to official ideology. The students learn what is incorrect behavior. They also learn what are incorrect ideas. Negativism, as ideologically incorrect ideas and behavior, is presently directly in the training, to be condemned; or is condemned when it appears indirectly in the response of the students.

NOTES

1. Tema (lit. 'theme') has a technical meaning in ideological training in Romania. In the

123

phrase <u>dans cu tema</u> (lit. dance with theme), <u>tema</u> refers to an item in official ideology.

2. Field Notes, October, 1973, Focal Unit of research.

3. Field Notes, November, 1973, Secondary Unit of research.

4. 'Big' and 'Small', here sound like pidgin English. <u>Tata Mare</u> (lit. Big Father) can also mean grandfather. But when I asked the child if she meant <u>bunicul</u> (lit. grandfather), when she said <u>tata mare</u>, she said, 'No, Nicolae Ceausescu'.

5. Field Notes, October, 1973, Focal Unit of research. I heard different variations of the satirical 'Our Father'.

6. Field Notes, two in May, 1972, one in November, 1973, Focal and Secondary Units of research.

7. Field Notes, December, 1973, Secondary Unit of research.

8. Field Notes, November, 1973.

9. Field Notes, December, 1972, January, 1973, Focal Unit of research.

10. Field Notes, February, 1975, Focal Unit of research.

11. Field Notes, December, 1972.

12. Field Notes, December, 1973, Focal Unit of research.

13. Field Notes, May, 1974, Secondary Unit of research.

14. Field Notes, January, 1975, Secondary Unit of research.

124

15. Ibid.

16. I asked 'who' to obtain membership. I reject-
    ed 'what is a family', 'what is your family',
    as being philosophically and linguistically
    bizarre questions for four and five year
    olds. However the 'who' may have prejudiced
    the answer. Field Notes, January-March,
    1975.

17. Field Notes, February, 1975, Focal Unit of re-
    search.

18. Field Notes, May, 1974.

19. Patriotic poetry is traditional in Romanian
    folklore. The Communist Party in the '50's
    was against traditional patriotic folklore;
    now the CP is an advocate of patriotism in
    every form.

20. Field Notes, October, 1975; interviewee in a
    general category.

21. I am using the model of en soi/pour soi (Ex-
    istence that is independent/dependent), used
    by Sartre. see: Jean-Paul Sartre, Being and
    Nothingness. trans. Hazel E. Barnes. New
    York: Philosophical Library, 1956.

22. Field Notes, April, 1973.

23. Not to be serios (lit. serious) in Romanian at
    the child level implies being silly, talking,
    and laughing out of turn, being mildly hyper-
    active.

24. Field Notes, 1974-1975. The Five Year Plan is
    the economic target over a period of five
    years.

25. Palita Silvestru, "The Pioneers' activities
    during the 20 years since the settling up of
    the Pioneers Organization" in National Sympo-
    sium, Bucharest 23-24, May, 1969.

26. Field Notes, March, 1973, Focal Unit of research.

27. M. Ralea, R. Hariton, The Sociology of Success. (Bucuresti: Editura Stintifica, 1962),
p. 524. Quoted in: National Symposium
(Bucharest 23-24, May, 1969), pp. 34-5.

28. Randolph L. Braham, Education in Romania,
(U.S. Government Printing Office, Washington;
1972), p. 33.

29. Anca Paunescu, "Civic Education--The Essential
Component of the Pioneers Activities", in
National Symposium, p. 72.

30. Quoted in National Symposium, p. 50.

31. Field Notes, April, 1974, Secondary Unit of
research.

32. Field Notes, September, 1974, Focal Unit of
research.

33. Field Notes, November, 1974, Secondary Unit of
research.

34. Field Notes, June, 1975, Focal Unit of research.

CHAPTER V

IDEOLOGICAL TRAINING IN THE HIGH SCHOOL
AND UNIVERSITY

Part I: The Academic High School

The student on graduating from Grade School,
chooses an academic-type High School (Liceu), if
the student wants to enter a University department
on finishing High School. The type of department
the student wants to enter determines for the most
part the choice of High School. If a student
wants to enter the English department, for example, the student chooses a High School of the
Humanities rather than one of the real sciences;
the High School will have a strong English program or be a school that concentrates on English.
Each academic High School has units of real science and humanities; the real science type school
has more hours of science per week than the humanities type school and the humanities type school
has more hours of humanities per week than the
real science type school. The High School student
in Romania throughout the four years follows a
multi-subject program similar to an American type
High School. There is no two-subject concentration in the last two years of High School as there
is traditionally in England.

The academic concentration in Romania is
achieved by the system of private tuition. I
could not get exact figures for the numbers of
students in High School who have private tuition.
But the fact that, in a University department,
more than 90% of the freshmen had had private
tuition in their four years of High School, would
give credence to a conclusion that students who
are serious about entering the University do have
private tuition. Teachers in High School told me
it is almost impossible to enter the University
without private tuition; University professors
confirmed this. Of the ten High School teachers
interviewed from the Focal Unit of research, all

gave private tuition to High School and Grade School students; of the twenty-five professors in the University department, twenty-four gave private tuition to High School students. Each University department since 1973 gives four hours a week of instruction during the academic year to students who intend sitting for the entrance examination in that department. The Ministry of Education ordered each department to give such 'instruction'.[1]

The High School student has the following weekly curriculum:

(a) Thirty hours of classroom attendance, with an average of four hours of homework per day.[2]

(b) Attendance at meetings of the Union of Communist Youth, four hours per week.

(c) (Possibly), Private tuition, with classes and homework.[3]

(d) (Possibly), Attendance at the four hours of instruction on Sundays at a University department.

The University freshmen surveyed in 1974 said they had devoted 10-12 hours per day in High School to school-connected work which would correspond to the total of (a), (b), (c), and (d) above.

The ideological training must be understood in the context of the whole situation because, unless a student gets a passing grade in discipline and ideological studies, he or she fails, and cannot achieve upward mobility through the High School. In the University entrance examination, students with the highest grades in the academic and ideological sections of the examination enter the department. The students' High School grades for discipline are also considered in the awarding of entry into a University department.

Part II: Ideological Training in the High School

The ideological training in the High Schools is carried out in the following ways: (a) Through the organization of the Union of Communist Youth; (b) in formal classes; (c) in the home-room; (d) in the history and literature classes; (e) through multiple-type work engagements.

Section 1: The Union of Communist Youth

All students in the High School are members of the Union of Communist Youth (UCY), the front organization which comes under the administration of the Central Committee of the Romanian Communist Party. Within a school, the UCY is governed by a committee which consists of officers from each of the Grades IX-XII. Grades in High School in Romania are counted as I-IV, but I will use the numbers IX-XII for ease of discussion and comparison with Grade School. Each grade elects its own officers. The candidates for election are proposed by the faculty who have responsibility for the UCY in the school. A faculty member who is both a member of the Party and an activist of the Party in the school, is appointed by the Director of the school on the advice of the Party Secretary of the faculty Party cell, to be responsible for one grade. A faculty member, usually the assistant to the Party Secretary of the faculty cell, is responsible for the UCY in the school. The Committee of the UCY in a school consists of one student from each class in each grade, one faculty member for each grade and one faculty member who has the overall responsibility for the UCY in the school. The Party Secretary of the school usually attends Committee meetings also.

Officially, a senior student is the President of the UCY in the school but the President acts under the supervision and direction of the faculty members who sit on the Committee of the UCY. The student members of the Committee of the UCY also sit on the Faculty Council of the school which is comprised of the Director of the school and heads of departments.

Officially, the UCY is a front organization whose function is to ensure participation in Party mobilization for individuals who are not members of the Party. In Romania, participation in a front organization is called participatory democracy. In the case of the UCY, participation entails obligatory attendance of all students at all general UCY weekly meetings. The general UCY meetings are presided over by the Committee of the UCY. The Director, the Assistant Director of the school and the Party Secretary of the school attend the general weekly meetings.

The weekly meetings have two distinct parts, criticism and ideological lectures. Any members of the student or faculty body present may criticize anyone or any group, student, staff, or faculty in the school, for ideologically incorrect behavior. The criticism may come from the floor or by previous letter to the UCY Committee; the letter may be signed or anonymous. Anonymous letters, if they are to be used in the UCY, must not be printed or typed. The following are examples[4] of criticism of students by the faculty: the appearance of students in the school is decadent because of short skirts or hair hanging over the face for girls; long hair for boys is decadent.

Male and female students wear school uniforms. In the High Schools I have seen very short skirts on girls and very long hair on boys. Criticism of appearance is intense usually for only two short periods in the school year; the periods of intense school criticism of appearance is matched by similar criticism of appearance of youth in general in the media.

Individual students or particular groups are criticized for using the titles Mr., Miss, and Mrs. in addressing faculty, instead of the title, Comrade. Students sometimes criticize individual faculty for failing to insist on the title Comrade when they are addressed by students. Faculty

sometimes criticize students for their sexual behavior such as holding hands and kissing in the
neighborhood of the school. Or, the criticism
will be of students' dress and sexual behavior
outside the school. Sex is a taboo subject in Romanian schools at all levels; this extends to verbal or overt behavior.

Faculty sometimes criticize students for
their lack of enthusiasm in actively promoting the
cause of the Party, or for paying lip service to
the cause without meaning it in their heart. The
faculty criticism of students sometimes follows a
media blitz in content. The fall of 1972, in the
UCY meetings at the Focal Unit of research, saw
an attack on students who are negligent in their
enthusiasm for the Party. The media in early 1972,
was constantly criticizing the motivation of ideological behavior in Romania: that people were
operating as hypocrites, operating as if they were
faithful to the Party but not believing in their
heart.

Student criticism of students at UCY meetings
includes behavior inside and outside the school.
Examples of criticism are: the trafficking in
black market goods from the West, such as ciga-
rettes and clothes; dressing in provocative
clothes; smoking and drinking; girls dating foreigners; talking in a derogatory manner about official doctrines, practices, or people in official
positions.

Criticism in the UCY meetings, is an important part of the ideological training in the High
Schools for four reasons. The students learn both
what is acceptable and what is not acceptable.
Through the criticism the students are exposed to
negativism or what is opposed to the official doctrine. Secondly, through the sanctions imposed on
individuals or groups as a result of criticism,
students learn that ideologically incorrect behavior can be sanctioned. Sanctions range from a
verbal dressing down to punishment by low grades,
or even expulsion. Thirdly, because of criticism,

131

students learn that public behavior is potentially observed at all times and therefore sanctionable. Fourthly, if students want to be considered as ideological activists, they are expected to engage in criticism of their peers, at least in a generic manner. Criticism of peers is also a part of the Party meeting agenda.

Student criticism of faculty is rare. In an interview with a group of faculty from different High Schools in July 1974,[5] I was told that student criticism of faculty occurs, for example, when there is an orchestrated campaign in the school against a particular faculty member. The campaign is initiated by individual faculty, or by the faculty who are members of the Party. The following example was given. A female teacher had gotten engaged to a foreigner. A group of students criticized the teacher for a lack of patriotism in deserting her country and her duty to students; at a later meeting the student leader of the UCY accused the teacher of treason. The teacher had been a member of the Party, which made her behavior more incorrect. The same group of teachers said that it was the possibility of anonymous criticism which made the practice of criticism important in the ideological training: you never know from whom, for what or when, the criticism might come for you.

The second part of the ideological training at the UCY meetings is the lecture. The ideological lecture may have one part or many; students may give the lectures, or faculty members who attend the UCY meetings. The topics are chosen by the faculty member responsible for the UCY in the school. If students read a part or all of a lecture, a faculty member will have directed the writing of the text. The text of all lectures to be delivered at UCY meetings must be submitted to the faculty member responsible for the UCY. Only texts that contain a stamp of approval from the UCY Committee can be read at the UCY meetings.

At every UCY meeting, there is a lecture.

The lecture deals with something topical which is
also being featured in the Party newspaper. Examples are: aspects of the Party or State decrees
and decisions, Party or State activities including
the economic life of the country; or foreign affairs, and Romania's policy about relations with
other countries. Examples of titles of lectures[6]
given at UCY meetings are the following:

'The student in a Multilaterally Developed Society.'

'Ceausescu and Peace.'

'Relations between Nations.'

'The Role of the Arts in a Socialist Society.'

Some of these topics include some aspects of
Nicolae Ceausescu's contribution to the development of ideology in the Marxist-Leninist tradition; the contribution of President Ceausescu is
frequently acknowledged during the lecture. He
becomes the source of authoritative statement.

Some of the President's ideas as contained in
these lectures are as follows. The concept of
'integrated' refers to the integration of school,
work, and organizational activity as the best
means of education; that education cannot be simple academic schooling. Peace in the relationship
between nations depends on the non-interference of
one nation or group of nations in the internal affairs of another nation. There must be total disarmament, especially nuclear disarmament and the
abolition of all military alliances. The artist,
writer, painter, sculpter, musician, or actor,
must contribute to the social progress of the nation by contributing to the planned development
as conceived by the Party in the dictatorship of
the proletariat; the artist cannot exist as an individual pursuing his own goals, or goals that are
in opposition to the good of society. The true
artist works in a social manner, creating in his
or her medium an artistic representation of the
goals of society and the Party.

The UCY also organizes the cultural life of
the school which includes cultural evenings, featuring patriotic and Party themes. As in the case
of the Pioneers, the UCY organizes competitions
and cultural events, on the school, district, municipality, county, and national level. Cultural
events and competitions include poetry, prose
stories and essays, music and songs, and art and
drama which have patriotic and Party themes. Cultural evenings are, like UCY meetings, outside
school hours. In the High School the patriotic
and Party lyrics are accompanied by light or folk
music usually with guitar accompaniment. On the
national level, well-known actors with pop and
folk singers stage concerts designed for and attended by UCY members; the concerts are frequently
televised. The emphasis at cultural events is
more on patriotism than Party themes, but sometimes the Party/State decisions and activities are
moulded in a patriotic framework. The Party,
State, and Nation are unified in the leadership of
the President who is the Secretary General of the
Party, the President of the State and a peasant
who went to jail for the Party and the country.
On most occasions, the President will be the dominant theme, as patriot or communist.

As in the case of the Pioneers' organization,
the UCY also organizes the attendance of High
School students at demonstrations. The High
School students attend all demonstrations in their
school uniforms. The kinds of demonstrations attended by High School students are the same kind
attended by the Pioneers. The High School students, especially the Juniors and Seniors, attend
more demonstrations than the Pioneers because the
UCY also goes to demonstrations late in the evenings. Faculty who are not responsible for the
UCY in a school, also accompany the High School
students as supervisors at demonstrations. Attendance at cultural events and demonstrations is
not optional for students or designated faculty.

Section 2: Special Classes in Ideology

Juniors and Seniors in High School have special classes on ideology. Students in Grade XI have at least two hours per week of Political Economy; students in Grade XII have two hours of Marxism and Philosophy and one hour of Psychology. Political Economy studies the role of economic progress in a Socialist State which is on the way towards a Communist State. This study involves the theoretical framework for the examination of the dynamics of a state controlled economy, where ownership of the means of production is not in private control; the control of industry, services, and agriculture as socialist phenomena, in the Marxist-Leninist tradition, signal the advancement of Socialism over Capitalism which is the step behind Socialism in the Marxist continuum. Capitalism is a primitive form in the evolution of history; capitalism is the exploitation by a small group of people who profit from the labor of the working class. The study of political economy also includes a study of Romania's social and economic progress since 1938.

The study of Marxism and Philosophy has three parts. There is a brief study of the general history of Philosophy. Secondly, key ideas in Marxism-Leninism are studied, such as internationalism through the brotherhood of the proletariat, alienation, the dictatorship of the proletariat, the role of the Party in the state as the voice of the people under Socialism, and the dialectic of history which creates different classes under capitalism which are mutually antagonistic. Under Socialism, antagonism disappears with the removal of the class structure which is created only by a capitalist system. Religion is a myth used by the exploiters to subdue the working classes with the false promise of future happiness which can be earned by suffering and deprivation in this life.

The study of Marxism in Grade XII, thirdly, includes the original contribution of President Nicolae Ceausescu to the doctrine of Marxism-

Leninism. One of the principles of the President's approach to Communist ideology is that Marxist-Leninism must be constantly reinterpreted in the light of development and new experience.

An important part of the President's ideology is that people will only accept an ideology in conscience, through means that are suitable as persuasion. In a speech at a plenary meeting of the Central Committee of the Romanian Communist Party in 1968, the President said: "History shows that no ideology can be imposed by decree or by force."[7] Ideas belong to the realm of the mind and the conscience, which can be reached only by practical participation in politics and persuasion.

The students read as homework selected abstracts from Marx, Engels, and Lenin. But the principal reading is from the speeches of the President which are published in the Party newspaper, Scinteia, and in pamphlet and book form. The teacher lectures in Grades XI and XII. Students are required to write essays as homework. Discussion in class is limited to positive reinforcement. In my observations, I never heard, from the faculty or students, negative questions or questions that presume non-committment to the official viewpoint. Students have tests and examinations on the material studied in the special classes on ideology in Grades XI and XII; the students are graded in the tests and examinations. The material of these classes also forms the basis for the ideological component in the entrance examination to each department of the University. The students learn by heart extracts from the speeches of Nicolae Ceausescu; direct quotation is required in the High School and the University entrance examinations.

The information in this section was gathered by observation and interview over the period 1972-1976. Some High School students said they also had private tuition in their last two years to prepare them for the ideological component of the

University entrance examination; some High School
students said they did not have private tuition
because preparing for the examination involved only learning the texts by heart.

Section 3: The Home-room

All students in High School have at least one
hour a week of home-room, with a teacher assigned
for the year as their home-room teacher. The
home-room in the High School functions similarly
to the home-room in Grades V-VIII. The teacher
makes administrative announcements such as times
for UCY meetings. The home-room teacher also controls the appearance of the students. In some
home-room sessions, I heard heated discussions and
complaints from the students about the rules restricting the dress, hair style, and use of make-
up for 17-19 year olds. Some teachers do not allow such discussions. The period of my research
coincided with the period of the popularity in Romania of the mini and micro skirt and the long
skirt after 1974; and also the period of long hair
for males. Nail polish was applied after school,
to be taken off before school. Some home-room
teachers did not object to make-up but the home-
room teacher is held responsible for a student in
his or her class, if another teacher reports a
student for wearing nail polish in school. Teachers and students in interviews stressed the ab-
surdity arising from the discrepancy between the
school definition of maturity and the social and
biological facts of life.

In the spring of 1974, in the society at
large, new rules were imposed which were never
published as decrees or laws. People over thirty-
five holding responsible positions must marry or
lose their jobs; living 'in sin' is punishable by
expulsion from the Party or is a cause from non-
admission. Being divorced or seeking a divorce is
a sign of ideologically incorrect behavior, as in
engaging in sex outside marriage. In the schools
where I did research, there were many instances of
compliance with the new directions regulating the

137

moral life. There were hurried marriages; petitions for divorce were withdrawn. Divorced people were refused membership of the Party. If allowed to enter, divorcees were investigated and criticized extensively before entry; their probationary period had a marriage proviso attached.

In the fall of 1974, the rules about the appearance of students were strictly enforced in the High Schools. When I interviewed female students and faculty outside of school whom I had previously met in school, sometimes I did not recognize them because of the change from their official to their social appearance.

The home-room teacher is also responsible for ideological instruction in the form of current events. In all classes where I observed the home-room, the teachers read to the students from newspapers, either Scinteia or Scinteia Tineretului, the edition of Scinteia for the youth. Students in Grades IX and X had to write a weekly essay on a current ideological topic for the home-room teacher. The home-room teacher for Grades IX-XII is consulted by the Academic Council of the school twice a year, when a grade is given each student for general behavior; the teachers of each student are also consulted by the Academic Council. It is however, the Academic Council which awards the grade for discipline.

Section 4: Ideology in the Literature and History Classes

The teaching of history in the High School follows the same pattern as the Grade School. For the first three years, world history is studied, covering the periods ancient, medieval, and modern. In the twelfth grade, Romanian history is studied. In the High School, the history is studied in more depth than in the Grade School. For example, all the heroes mentioned in Section 2, Part II or Chapter III, are dealt with.

In the section on Romanian history the key

ideas of Nicolae Iorga are studied in Grade XII.[8]
Nicolae Iorga is now regarded as Romania's National historian and has become an official Hero. The Institute of History at the Academy is named after him. He was a prolific writer of history whose philosophy of history was a nationalistic one. Iorga was on the prohibited list in the first years of the communist regime in Romania because of his nationalism, even though he had been murdered by fascists in 1940. The key ideas in Iorga are: (a) a people is the product of its past; (b) Romanian nationalism is cultural and ethnic and is the product of pamintul romanesc (lit., the Romanian earth); (c) a nation is a group of people united by one suflet (lit., mind and spirit) which produces the patria (lit., the fatherland) and the neamuri (lit., the national people and family); (d) tara (lit., country) is the object of a man's allegiance.

These ideas of Iorga and more especially, their wording, have become an important part of the official ideology in Romania in the Ceausescu era. Iorga's philosophical framework for the study of history has been adopted officially in the Romanian School of historical study.

The study of literature has two sections. The theory of literature is studied and actual works of literature are studied.

In the theoretical study, the official ideology for all literature and all art has two parts. Firstly, art and writing must belong to social realism; secondly, the writer and the artist must be participants in the Socialist state, as the creative arm of the Party and its leaders in the edification of the people. Artists and writers as the messengers of the ethic of Socialist humanism, act as the reinforcement of the political and moral unity of all the people. The writer, the artist, and the composer show their common source of inspiration by signalling in their works the end of man's exploitation by man, the end of social injustices and the emergence of the new man in

139

Socialism who works for the good of the collective, and society, and the fatherland.

Social realism then does not mean the portrayal of society as it is. The negative aspect of the theory shows this more clearly. The moral man must be portrayed; the true artist does not deal with pornography. I tried in many interviews to find out what is meant by pornography. In general, homosexuality, lesbianism, the portrayal of the sexual act in either usual or unusual ways, the portrayal of the genitalia and the portrayal of the heterosexual sex act outside marriage are all considered as pornographic.

Pornography is part of the negative trilogy, which includes pessimism and mysticism. Pessimism has two parts. Anything which portrays the unpleasant side of life such as mental illness, depression, abortion is considered pessimistic; also included as pessimistic is anything which does not portray the glorious advancement of the new Socialist man, such as child abuse or wife-beating. The latter part gives pessimism wide-ranging application.

Mysticism was a difficult concept to research. Although not stated officially, mysticism is limited in its denotation. It does not always apply, for example, to patriotism or nationalism; the adaption of Iorga's framework as the official framework for the portrayal of nationalism and patriotism could be considered mystical for example. Examples of mysticism given me were: any kind of religious framework, be it of an organized religion with belief in a supreme deity or a philosophy such as Zen; the positing of any cause outside the framework of material consequence such as some aspects of motivation in Freudianism.

However, the study of actual writings in Romanian and world literature includes works of a mystical nature and some pessimism. Romanian writers from before the war are studied. Lucian Blaga, for example, was a poet who used Indian

philosophy as a primary source. Octavian Goga
was mildly fascist. But because both are great
Romanian poets, they are studied, despite their
negative elements.

In the High School, contemporary Romanian
literature is studied. Much of contemporary Romanian poetry is highly symbolic and mystical;
some of it mildly pessimistic. The contemporary
novel and drama, for the most part, obeys the can-
ons of social realism without pornography (in the
Romanian sense), pessimism or mysticism; some
symbolism and mysticism do appear in patriotic
sections of novels and drama. Foreign works are
studied such as Tolstoy, Dostoevsky, Camus, and
Shakespeare.

In general, it can be said that the ideological training in the theory of literature, is
somewhat ignored in the actual study of literature and some of the contemporary literature.
Sex of any kind or degree, is avoided as much as
possible; this is in keeping with the treatment of
sex in the school and the society in general,
where it is a taboo.

In the contemporary Romanian society, poetry
is very popular; young poets are national figures.
Students in High Schools write poetry for class
exercises and private pleasure; the poetry I read
from High School students was highly symbolic.
Poetry using social realism as a model is written
primarily for public competition in poetry; poetry
written for competition or as a class exercise is
supposed to be in the model of social realism in
the praise of Socialist humanism. In the display
classes for teachers from High Schools, I taught
contemporary American, British, and Irish poetry
which was sometimes mystical and pessimistic; I
taught display lessons to High School students
using the works of the same poets. In practice
then, the ideology as it pertains to writing, is
largely confined to the contemporary Romanian novel and drama, not to poetry, or the readings of
world literature with some notable exceptions such

141

as the works of Henry Miller, which are forbidden because of the sexual explicitness.

Section 5: Ideological Training Through Work

There are three categories of work, patriotic, productive and practical. Patriotic work is work of any kind which does not require special skills or training, such as cleaning the ground, digging the earth, picking fruit or potatoes and non-artistic painting. Students in the Kindergarten and Grade School have some patriotic work such as cleaning; in the countryside Grade School students also have patriotic work in the fall, at harvest time. Productive work is work in a factory, for example, where there is actual production such as making plastic utensils or machine tools. Faculty accompany students on patriotic work and productive work. Practical work is work directly connected with the material studied in school. For example, students in a High School of real science which concentrates in chemistry and biology, may do work in a laboratory or factory where chemistry and biology are applied in a practical way.

In general, during the research period, High School students fulfilled their work engagements through patriotic work. But in the period 1974-1976, there was an increasing trend of High School students also doing productive and practical work.

Patriotic work is generally geared to meeting needs of the moment such as cleaning and painting the school, planting trees, cleaning areas before demonstrations and Presidential visits, helping with the harvesting of fruit and vegetables in the fall. Faculty supervise the patriotic work of students. I also noticed a trend that the more prestigious the High School, academically and socially, the less the patriotic work done by the students. Faculty and administrators told me the Director of the school was the key figure; the more influential the Director, the less the patriotic work done by students in the school.

142

In the 1974-1976 period, when faculty and
Party meetings were discussing and seeking ways to
implement the directive of 'integral education',
there seemed to be emerging a trend whereby lack
of work engagement in a school would be considered as lack of enthusiasm for official ideology and
directives. This could cause an increase in the
work engagement in High Schools, in the future.

Productive and practical work was not done in
all of the High Schools which served as the Focal
and Secondary units of research. In the three
High Schools which had productive and practical
work engagements, productive work was for a half-
day a week outside of school hours; the curriculum
remained the same. When productive work had been
introduced, it was added to the curriculum with
the time given to academic work remaining the
same. The three High Schools where I did observation, went to a plastics factory, a machine tool
factory, and a knitting factory. The students received little or no training; at the factory they
watched the line workers, helping with cleaning
and sometimes passing things to the line workers.
At the plastics factory, the students sometimes
helped the packers. The students were an addendum
at the factory, never initiating work or doing
work independently. The factories had not asked
for student help; no steps had been taken at the
factories to integrate the students. The plastics
factory workers enjoyed the presence of young la-
dies; some foremen told me it was all 'politics',
with production figures actually falling when students, for example, helped in packing because regular workers had to take time out from their own
work to show students, undo mistakes made by students and help them do the job right.

Examples of practical work were working in a
laboratory and in various offices of different
Ministries. Practical work is done in concentrated periods such as two to four weeks in the summer. In practical work on the High School level,
students were added to the work force; no new jobs
were started for the students. The students were

not required to fulfill work quotas. In the practical work, students were not accompanied by faculty from the school. A general report was made by an administrator at the place of work to the Director of the School. Faculty sometimes visited the sites where practical work was being done by their students.

Part III: The University Department

The University is divided into Faculties which are sub-divided into Departments. There is a Dean and an Associate Dean in each faculty; a Department is administered by a Department head who is the professor who holds the chair (sef de catedra). Faculty are also categorized according to rank; the main division is between faculty who give lectures and faculty who only hold seminars. Individual students do not have advisers or tutors; groups of students have a home-room teacher.

Students do most of their academic work within a department concentrating on their major; most students have a minor which is connected in some way with their major. For example, students majoring in chemistry often minor in biology rather than, for example, in a foreign language. When a student enters a department, he or she is assigned to a seminar group of usually fifteen students. The student stays with this seminar group for the whole four years of undergraduate work. The group attends lectures with other groups. Each group has a student leader who is appointed by the Faculty Council. The student leader of a seminar group marks the group roll book for each seminar or lecture period; the faculty member taking the seminar or lecture counter signs the roll book or books. In general, the group leader is the liaison between administration, faculty, the students' unions, and the seminar group. The home-room teacher stays with a group during the four years of undergraduate study but does not engage in ideological training.

In 1971, the period of undergraduate study

144

was reduced from five to four years. In the research period I was able to follow two batches of students through their undergraduate work.

The primary emphasis on the undergraduate level in Romanian universities, as in most other European universities, is on teaching rather than research. The minimum number of contact hours for students in any department is thirty per week. The trend during the five years was towards increasing the number of contact hours. Because one day a week in each department is devoted to military training for female students, on some days students, can have 8-10 contact hours. If there is a meeting of the Union of Communist Youth on a particular day, students are sometimes in a department from 8 A.M. to 8 P.M., with one half-hour break for lunch.

On entering a department as a freshman, a student signs a contract promising to obey all the rules and regulations of the University and the department. The student also has a contractual agreement which obliges the student to work for three years after graduation wherever the Government decides; the nature of the job will be in general conformity with the course of study pursued by the graduate in university.

The appointment to a job for three years by the Government at graduation, has an important effect on the ideological training in the university department. The place and nature of appointment depends inter alia on grade point average, which includes the grades for ideology and discipline; the appointment also depends on political activism during the four years of study. Students are concerned about this appointment, even in their freshman year. Of 350 freshmen in three years, 1973-1975, less than 5% wanted appointments to places other than Bucharest. In the July appointments by the Government in 1975, only 10% of the graduates of one department were appointed to positions in Bucharest. Only one out of the twelve who made up this 10% belonged to the top 10% in academic

145

grades. Five of the twelve were political activists as members of the Communist Party. The causal relationship between political activism and favorable appointments is not one invented by me. Students in their sophomore year, for example, said to me they were pursuing an activist role in the hope of getting a Bucharest appointment. In discussions with students and faculty, I expressed surprise at most people wanting a position in a large city. The stereotype about life in the provinces is that social life consists of a poker game between the teacher, the doctor, the engineer, and the priest. The girls were worried about their marriage prospects being restricted to a local tractorist (tractor driver in the collective or state farm). Legal residence is also restricted by official job appointment which may involve a girl being married to a man in Bucharest, while she has an appointment in a village hundreds of miles away which determines her legal domicile. But probably the reason most students wanted to stay in Bucharest after graduation was the lack of cultural and social services in the provinces.

It is not my concern here to describe how people cope with avoiding leaving Bucharest after graduation but the fact that the appointment after graduation can depend on grades received in the classes on ideology and on practical activism during the four years of undergraduate study, is important.

When the student enters a university department, he or she is given a grade book (carnet), and a student's identification card (legitimatia) which entitles the student to legal residence in Bucharest. In the grade book are entered the grades received for each subject at the examinations at the end of each semester; the grade at graduation is an accumulated grade average. The student must have these two documents on his or her person at all times. If a student receives a private written disciplinary warning, or a written disciplinary warning which is published on the official bulletin board of the department, the warning is entered officially in the last pages of the grade book. Disciplinary warnings are issued for different kinds of reasons such as absences, disobedience towards administrators, faculty or student officers, or ideologically incorrect behavior. Rewards are also given students and recorded in the grade book. Rewards are given for such things as high grades and political activism. Rewards are sometimes monetary, or, for example, access to special privileges such as reserved accommodation in the mountains or at the seaside during the vacations.

Part IV: Ideological Training in the University

Ideological training through work engagements and organizations becomes more important in the University than in other educational institutions. There is also ideological training in formal classes on ideology; there is also, as in the High School, training through attendance at demonstrations and cultural events. What is unique however to the University is ideological training through military service.

Section 1: Military Service

Male students since 1973 are expected to have completed their compulsory military service before entering University. Before 1973, male University students did their military service after graduation. I am not reporting on the military service of males, because it happens completely outside of the context of education. In the latter half of the research period the male students entering the University had already completed their military training. Male students brought the training to my attention without being asked because one item in the training concerned me.

The same item comes up in the military training of female students. Female students fulfill their compulsory military service by doing their military training for one day per week during the semester and four weeks during the summer vacation from the University. I did not observe the training of the female students. The students told me they would never speak to me again if I ever came to see them in military uniform. They were not joking. Students in the University do not wear school uniforms; one of the worst memories University students, both male and female, have of High School is the compulsory wearing of school uniforms. Male and female students had a similar distaste for all uniforms.

But the principal reason for not observing military training was that it was impossible. In the first lesson in ideology on the first day of military training, the students are told that all foreigners who drive cars in Romania are spies. Male and female students thought it was very amusing that I was automatically a spy because I was an Irishman who drove a car. I was raised myself in a very pacifist home in a country which does not have compulsory military service. I find it difficult to realize military service actually happens anywhere. What I am reporting about the ideological training of the female students is purely from interviews.

Some of the young army officers who are responsible for the military training of female University students, are people who failed to get into the University. The University students continually complained in interviews that the young officers gave them a hard time because of jealousy.

Some of the military training consists of drilling, marching, and firing practice. There is also ideological training. There is one formal period of one hour and a half during each day of military training. The three themes of the ideological training are nationalism and devotion to the President and the Party. Negativism is also included. Negativism includes: lack of devotion to the President, the country, or the Party; the adoption of foreign tastes or styles; any contact with foreigners of any kind, either capitalists or foreigners from neighboring countries. The President is now Supreme Commander of the armed forces. Nicolae Ceausescu, himself a graduate of the Military Academy had been in the early '50's the director of the political department of the army while he was assistant minister of defense with the rank of lieutenant-general. Ideological training is an important part of the military training. Positive themes in the training include: readiness to work, fight and die for the fatherland; obedience to the orders of the President and the Party; anticipation of the wishes of the President; vigilance against people, be they Romanians or foreigners, who undermine the Party or the fatherland in any way; the duty of reporting ideologically incorrect behavior, verbal or overt; the importance of accepting criticism from officers and reforming oneself on the basis of the criticism.

While the ideological training is in the form of lectures, the content of the training is reinforced by the chanting by the students of slogans such as: "Ceausescu PCR" (the Romanian Communist Party), 'Romania, Romania', 'Long Live the Party', 'Long Live Romania'. The chanting takes place in the classroom and during drilling practice. Songs are sung during marching practice with themes of patriotism, nationalism, and themes extolling the President, the Party, Socialism, Communism, the army and fighting for the defense of the fatherland.

Lectures in the section on ideological training includes: the history of the Romanian army's defense of the fatherland in both world wars; the army's role in the defeat of the fascist forces in World War II and the army's cooperation with the armies of Socialism and Communism in the institution of the new order of Socialism in Romania in 1944.

Because the female students are soldiers of the Romanian army, their fraternization with foreigners is regarded as graver than the fraternization of other Romanians with foreigners. It is more difficult for female University students to obtain permission to marry foreigners, for example, than it is for females of the same age who are workers. Military service for females is compulsory only for female students in Higher Education. Female University students can avoid military service only for medical or psychological reasons; the army psychologists assess a student if a student claims inability to undergo military training because of psychological reasons.

Section 2: Ideological Training Through Organizations

All students in the University are members of the Union of Communist Youth (UCY). Meetings are held weekly. Usually the weekly meeting is organized by students in a particular year, unless the department is very small. In such cases all students in a department attend the same meeting. In the larger departments there are supplementary meetings, usually once a month, when all the students in a department meet at a department meeting of the UCY. Officers for the year-group are elected by the students of that group. Candidates for election as UCY officers are usually presented on the advice of faculty responsible for the UCY in the department. For a student to refuse candidacy when chosen by faculty, is regarded as a sign of lack of support for the Party. I heard of no refusal in the departments where I did research in the period 1971-1976. Students sometimes refuse to elect a proposed candidate and propose their own candidate. This happens rarely and usually only in the freshman year. The candidate proposed by students must receive the approval of faculty, if the candidate can be presented for election.

A candidate proposed by students may not receive approval by faculty for various reasons. Low academic grades, for example, low grades for discipline or warnings registered in the student's grade book can be reasons for non-approval by faculty. If the student comes from a family which was bourgeois before 1946 and opposed the new regime in any way in the middle and late '40's, the

150

student is unlikely to receive faculty approval
for candidacy for election. If the student comes
from a bourgeois family from before 1946 but which
has demonstrated its loyalty to the new regime
through Party activism, then the student can be
accepted for candidacy.

The faculty who are responsible for the UCY
in a department are usually junior faculty who, in
turn, are supervised by the head of the department,
the dean of the faculty and from the Party, the
Party Secretary, and the second officer of the
Communist Party in the department. A student from
the senior class who is an officer of the UCY is
the President of the UCY in the department; the
President is usually the President of the UCY in
his or her year group. Each year group has its
own President and officers. The Committee of the
UCY in a department is made up of the Presidents
of each year group, officers elected at a general
meeting of the UCY and faculty members responsible
for the UCY in the department. Heads of the department, the Party Secretary of the Department,
and the Party activist who is the second officer
of the Party, sometimes attend UCY meetings at all
levels; they attend all meetings which elect officers. They also attend when they are going to
give the ideological lecture at the UCY meeting.
Attendance at UCY meetings is obligatory for students.

The agenda of the weekly UCY meeting includes
criticism and ideological lectures. There may be
more than one lecture. Sometimes one to four students give short lectures; sometimes a faculty
member or an official from the Central Committee's
cadre of ideological training will give the lecture. Sometimes inspectors from the Central Committee attend the UCY meetings. At the UCY meetings, students are also told about upcoming cultural events and demonstrations. Attendance at
cultural events is not always obligatory; attendance at non-obligatory events is a sign of political activism.

Criticism at UCY meetings in the University
is similar to criticism at the UCY meetings in
High School. Faculty criticize students; students
criticize each other, individually or in groups.
Periodic group criticism on the University level
is usually a formality, unless the accusation is
about the students negative comments about the
Party or the President, for example. An example
of criticism as a formality would be the accusation of the lack of proper enthusiasm. Serious
negative criticism can bring investigation on the
department level; criticism such as the accusation
of negative comments about the President would also involve investigation by the security forces.

I had no certain way of finding out the depth
of the presence of the security forces in the
University. What is important for the description
of the ideological training in the University is
that students and faculty think the presence of
the security forces is prevalent. In practice,
the consciousness of being observed by the security forces influences the ideological behavior of
both faculty and students, verbal and overt; students form small trust groups which divides their
public behavior into two quite distinct kinds.
People in other societies also manifest quite distinct modes of public behavior. But in Romania
the two kinds of public behavior, in the trust and
non-trust group, are often contradictory. I am
not implying however, that the behavior in the
trust-group context is the true indicator of the
persons' belief and feeling. But it was important
for me to know when I was observing behavior in a
trust or a non-trust group context. Both the faculty and the students were always conscious of
being observed, unless they were in a trust-group
which is determined by social contact outside of
school.

Open student criticism of individual students
is, in the main, confined to such things as non-
attendance at UCY meetings, for example. Accusa-
tions of negative behavior such as derogatory comments about the Party are usually made by anonymous

letter which may be printed or typed. Open criticism of an individual of a serious nature, occurs usually when an individual student has applied for permission to marry a foreigner; open criticism would occur especially when the student in question is an officer of the UCY or a member of the Communist Party. The open criticism is necessary because faculty and Party officers could be accused of lack of vigilance in the investigation of the student before he or she had been proposed for candidacy as an officer of the UCY, or for membership of the Party. Student criticism of the individual student would be mobilized to show the shock and horror of the whole collective body, because of the unpatriotic act of the student. Engaging in open criticism of a student by a student is interpreted as a signal of political activism or political ambition.

Sometimes there is criticism, open or anonymous, of a student by another student or group of students, when the criticized student as a political activist, has been making life very unpleasant for other students. This example is a complicated case involving the isolation of the student in question before the criticism is made; if the student has a strong base with faculty and other student officers, or high political status through family membership, then the criticism could be turned back on the student or group of students making the criticism.

Faculty criticize students for such things as westernism. Westernism involves copying western styles of appearance for example, or regarding western culture as superior to Romanian culture. Students are criticized for attending Western libraries, and Western cultural events which are not directly sponsored by the Romanian Government. Students are criticized for their attendance at coffee bars, bars, and night clubs.

The criticism of students by faculty and officers of the UCY often follows trends in the society. The attack on Westernism among students

153

was strong in the fall and winter of 1972-1973.
In his address, officially opening the 1972-'73
academic year in September 1972 at the University
of Cluj, President Nicolae Ceausescu had condemned
the slavish imitation of western youth who were
destroying everything sacred in society. During
the period of research, most of the coffee bars
within walking distance of University departments
were abolished; discos in Bucharest were abolished.
Coffee bars and discos waste students' time and
foster hooliganism. Students were reported to the
department by police who check identity cards in
coffee bars; faculty would then criticize the students at UCY meetings.

Lectures at UCY meetings are usually topical,
dealing with decrees of the Central Committee and
in general following the main articles in the
Party newspaper, Scinteia and Scinteia Tineretului.
For example, in 1974, there were lectures about:
the appointment of Nicolae Ceausescu to the newly
created office of the Presidency; about the visits
of Nicolae Ceausescu abroad to Arab, African, and
South American countries. The National Party Congress took place in the fall of 1974; most of the
lectures at the UCY meetings for the first semester of 1974-'75 dealt with the preparation for the
Congress and the documents published during and
after the Congress.

The lectures at UCY meetings deal in general,
with Romanian phenomena, not with Marxist-Leninism
or other such theoretical items unless they are
the speeches of Nicolae Ceausescu.

While all students are members of the UCY,
some students in the second, third, and fourth
years are invited to apply, or apply themselves
for membership in the Communist Party. Each department has its own branch of the Party. About
10% of the students in the second year are invited
to become members of the Party; additional numbers
are invited when a class is in the third and
fourth years. Students who apply for membership
without being invited invariably are refused entry;

154

their application is often postponed.

Invitations to apply for entry depend on the
political status of a student's family for example; a student whose father is a member of the
Central Committee is automatically invited to apply for membership. Some students who are officers of the UCY and hence considered as political activists, are invited to apply for membership. The system of inviting certain students to
apply for membership in the Communist Party is an
important part of the ideological training in the
University. The invitation is given only to a
maximum of 20% of students in years 2-4 of the
undergraduate training. Political activism in the
first and second years is rewarded by an invitation to join the Party. Being a member of the
Party before graduation is an accepted signal of
political activism and useful in obtaining a
Bucharest appointment.

The students in a department observe the process of students being invited to apply for entry
into the Communist Party, the process of students
entering the Party, and the obligations and benefits accruing from membership of the Party. The
students, from this experience, learn the practical implications of ideological training. The
Communist Party is the organization for adult Communists. The University department serves as the
place where students begin the rite of entry and
the ritual acceptance into the Party. Only students in Higher Education can enter the Party before the age of 25. Entry for students into the
Communist Party is easier than for faculty, for
example. If a faculty member is invited to apply
there is a thorough investigation of why he or she
did not enter earlier; the investigation of the
personal and professional behavior is also more
thorough for faculty than for student applicants.
It is a positive benefit then for a student to become a Party member before graduation.

The process of entering the Party involves
being investigated and being accepted by members

155

of the Party cell in the department. The investigation involves a study by a committee from the cell of the student's school record as contained in the student's dossier; a cross-examination of peers inquiring into the student's personal, moral, and political behavior. Examinations are not thorough; in practice, unless a Party member or a peer wants to impede entry, a student is accepted as a member of the Party. The entry of students is frequently postponed until the student shows more signs of political activism and enthusiasm in promoting the official ideology. The student will then be accepted on the second or third application.

Most students accept the invitation to apply to enter the Party even though it involves an extra four to six hours a week for attendance at the Party meeting. Being a member of the Party while a student helps at graduation in getting a post in Bucharest. There are also other advantages. Membership improves one's chance of getting a tourist visa to go abroad, either privately with a tourist group or officially with a student delegation. Since most graduates as members of the intellectual elite become, sooner or later, members of the Party, the students who joined the Party while undergraduates said one reason for joining was to enjoy early in life, the advantages of joining, which is inevitable in the long run for most of the intellectual elite.

It is important for Party members to sponsor new members; sponsoring new members is one way of showing one's political activism. But if something unsuitable, such as sexual activity outside marriage, should become known during the examination of the candidate or should the new member behave later in a manner unsuitable for Party members, then the original sponsor can be blamed for negligence, lack of vigilance, and bad judgment. For example, in 1975, a student member of the Party applied for a visa to go abroad permanently and for permission to marry a foreigner. The faculty member who had sponsored the student's candidacy for membership was investigated. Self-criticism, involving admission of lack of vigilance and bad judgment, sufficed as the faculty member's sanction. The student was formally expelled from the Party and the UCY; she was called a traitor and other rather obnoxious terms while she was criticized at various meetings of both the Party and the UCY. But the students learn from the system of sponsorship that individuals need sponsors if they are going to achieve acceptance into the adult community of official political activists in the Communist Party.

Section 3: Ideological Training Through Work Engagements

University students do patriotic, practical, and productive work. For example, students spend two to three weeks in the early fall harvesting fruit and vegetables; students clear river banks and other such tasks which are not regular. Helping with the harvest during three to four weeks in the Fall, is the regular patriotic work for students in most University departments.

University students usually do their practical work for two or three weeks at the beginning or the end of the second semester. For example, students who study foreign languages translate periodicals and books into Romanian or act as guides for tourists; engineering students work with the branches of the Department of Roads and Bridges.

Productive work is done in factories. Students from one department where I did research worked occasionally in a factory for canning fruit. Productive work is not done on a regular basis. In the last year of the research 1975-'76, with the increasing discussion at faculty meetings and in the media, of integrated education, plans were being drawn up to increase the amount of productive work done by students. The purpose of the productive work done by students was to increase production; but also to unite the intellectual

157

class with the workers. In 1975-'76, in the society at large, there was started the process of
having adults from the intellectual elite do periodic manual work.

The department is paid for practical work
done by students. The students receive no re-
numeration, for any work, patriotic, practical, or
productive. Students are given bed and board if
their work invovles being away from home.

Section 4: Formal Classes in Ideology

A special pool of faculty from the departments of political economy and philosophy, and
from the secretariat of the Central Committee of
the Communist Party which is responsible for propaganda, act as faculty for the classes in ideology throughout the University. Each year-group in
every department has a two-hour lecture a week;
each seminar group has a two-hour seminar each
week.

The content of the ideological classes is divided into three parts. The first part covers
Marxism-Leninism. The origins of the dialectic in
Hegel and the application of the dialectic in a
material context by Fuerbach is included in the
section on Marxist-Leninism. Other topics include: alienation, exploitation, the historical
evolution of material forces in feudalism, capitalism, Socialism, and Communism, the phenomenon
of the bourgeoisie, the dictatorship of the proletariat, the continuing revolution and the value
of labor. Students write a few short essays each
semester and have a graded examination at the end
of each semester. The course notes of the lectures constitute the material for the examinations.

The ideology classes also include the study
of the documents of the Romanian Communist Party
and the history of the Communist Party. However
it is the published speeches of Nicolae Ceausescu
which function as the focus of these two parts of
the ideological study. Topics include: the suprem-

acy of the Party in the political, economic, and
social life of the country; the right of all countries to develop according to their own needs,
without the interference of one country in the internal affairs of another; the multilateral development of Romania in the union of the political,
the spiritual, the social, the cultural, and the
moral; the family as the sacred unit of society.
Ethical topics include honesty, lack of selfish-
ness, hard work, enthusiasm, and devotion to the
President and the Party. The student fulfills the
work ethic by gaining a grade of nine or ten.

The ideological classes are in the form of
instruction: students receive information in class
and reproduce it in essays and examinations. The
key principles of the thoughts of Nicolae Ceausescu are printed on banners which adorn the walls of
every department.

Section 5: Ideological Training Through Cultural Events and Demonstrations

University students in departmental groups go
to the same demonstrations as the students in High
Schools. Sometimes demonstrations are during the
class times, sometimes outside school hours. Attendance at demonstrations is obligatory. Group
leaders take the attendance of students at demonstrations. At some demonstrations, students are
required to sing, dance, or take part in special
programs such as artistic marching formations; in
such cases there will be rehearsals.

Each year-group in a department periodically
holds a cultural event where attendance is obligatory. The students will recite poetry, sing songs
individually and in groups and perform short
dramas, which have patriotic and Party themes.
Love of and loyalty to, the President will frequently be incorporated as both patriotic and Party themes.

Nicolae Ceausescu's career and achievements
are celebrated. In the period immediately follow-

ing the war, Ceausescu became the Secretary of the Central Committee of the UCY and in 1945, at the age of twenty-seven, a member of the Central Committee of the Party. After various jobs in the provinces, he became Deputy Minister of agriculture at the age of thirty. As leader of the Party since 1965, he is also chairman of the commission which drew up the new constitution adopted by the Grand National Assembly in August 1965. He is now Secretary General of the Party; the First Secretary of the Party's Central Committee and member of the three ruling organs of the Party. He is not only President of the Republic but also President of the State Council. He is President of the Supreme Council of Economic and Social Development. He is the President of the Socialist Unity Front, the front party in the state sector. He is also the President of the Academy of Social and Political Sciences. In the fall of 1977, he also became chairman of the National Worker's Council.

A department as a whole, groups of departments, or the whole University will sometimes hold cultural events of a similar nature. Active participation in cultural events featuring patriotic and Party themes is regarded as a signal of political activism; non-attendance at such an event can cause a student to be accused of political negativism.

NOTES

1. Field Notes, October, 1973, Focal Unit of research, University Department.

2. From interviews with High School students in the three categories of research.

3. Of twenty senior High School students surveyed in 1973 and 1974, the average time for private tuition was four hours per week; homework for the private classes was at least four hours per week.

160

4. The information about the UCY was gathered in the years 1972-1976 from interviews with students and faculty.

5. Field Notes, July, 1974.

6. Field Notes. Topics are from different High Schools, including Focal and some Secondary Units of research in the period 1973-1976.

7. From the President's speech quoted in Michel-P. Hamelet, Nicolae Ceausescu (Paris: Seghers, 1971), p. 147.

8. See: William O. Oldson, The Historical and Nationalistic Thought of Nicolae Iorga. New York: Columbia University Press, 1973.

CHAPTER VI

THE IDEOLOGICAL TRAINING OF FACULTY

While the faculty are responsible for much of
the ideological training of the students and the
supervision of the ideological behavior of students, they themselves are also the subject of
ideological training. The ideological behavior of
faculty is also supervised: both their ideological
training of students is supervised and their own
personal behavior.

When teachers have completed three years of
teaching, they are candidates for a permanent
teaching license. Teachers in their first three
years are inspected by the district committee for
education. School inspectors visit the classrooms
and report on the teacher. Part of the report is
academic; part of it also deals with the teacher's
ability and success in imparting proper ideological attitudes to the students in the classroom.
The inspectors also report on the teacher's participation in the political activism of the institution: whether the teacher was active in the work
engagements of students and in the organizations
of the school such as the Pioneers, the UCY, and
the Communist Party; whether the teacher organized
cultural events featuring patriotic and Party
themes; whether the teacher in the home-room activities was successful in teaching ideology and
supervising the behavior of the students.

Upward mobility for a teacher who has received a permanent license, includes a substantial
salary increase; the increase depends upon the
teacher qualifying as a Grade I teacher after five,
and as a Grade II teacher after ten years experience. Both the Grade I and Grade II qualifications are dependent on a teacher following a series of courses at the Institute for the Perfecting of Teaching Faculty. The teacher attends
courses on the academic subjects, methodology, an
ideology. The teacher must also pass an examina-

tion in ideology. Independently of the special
courses for the Grade I and II examinations, all
teachers must undergo every five years a refresh-
er course which includes ideological training.
Teachers in schools also attend periodically,
special lectures on ideology arranged by the Party
at the district, municipal, and county levels.

But the principal ideological training and
supervision of faculty comes through the organizations of the school. The teacher attends Faculty and Trade Union meetings in the school; since
most faculty are also members of the Communist
Party, they attend Party meetings also.

In every educational institution, there is a
three-fold administration:

Type	Academic	Political	Trade Union
Head	Director	Party Secretary	Secretary of
	Dean		the Union
	Head of Department		

The dynamics of the relationship between the
three types of administration is complex. The
Secretary of the Trade Union usually does not dom-
inate in the wielding of administrative power.
The Secretary of the Union is always a Party member, but the Union as a front organization of the
Party, is subservient to the rule of the Party in
the school, in the person of the Party Secretary.

The role of the Director, chairman of a department, or Dean and the role of the Party Secretary of an institution are theoretically distinct.
But in practice, because of the lack of a clear-
cut distinction between academic and ideological
training, there sometimes is a clash between the
Director and the Party Secretary. This usually
happens when the Director has not been a Party
activist before becoming a Director.

In the '50's and '60's, the Director was usually a teacher trained before the advent of the

new regime; the Party Secretary was a young teacher who received his or her teacher training under the Communist regime. The Party Secretary was usually the chief administrator as the political representative and political supervisor. During the period of research, 1971-1976, many of the directors of institutions were people who had been themselves Party activists before becoming Directors; in this instance, the chief administrator in an institution is usually the Director who continues to act as a political activist.

In one University department where I did research, the chairman was in his late 50's, the Party Secretary in her 30's. In the department, the Party Secretary was the chief administrator. For example, purely academic awards only went to students who were also political activists. Promotion of faculty was measured primarily by activist criteria; faculty who were activists received the academic qualifications necessary for promotion while faculty who were not activists lost positions such as section chairman within the department.

In another faculty, the Dean had been a prominent political activist before being appointed as Dean. The Party Secretary was only his political assistant; decisions effecting the political training of students or faculty were made by the Dean with the Party Secretary acting as supervisor. But in academic appointments and promotion of faculty, the criteria used were primarily academic; in the granting of academic awards to students, both academic and political criteria were used. But students who were not political activists did receive some academic awards in the department.

In general, the intensity of the ideological training of faculty and students, is to some extent dependent on who the chief administrator is in the institution. The description which follows is a general account of the minimum ideological training received by faculty in an educational institution. All educational institutions, independently of whether the academic Director, Chairman, or Dean is the chief administrator, are assessed by the Party which inspects the ideological training and behavior of administrators, faculty, and students. The University is assessed by the Central Committee of the Party; other institutions are assessed by the Party at the district or the county level.

The Party Secretary of a school supervises the ideological training carried out by teachers in the school; the Party Secretary also supervises the ideological behavior of teachers. The following is a case study illustrating the supervision exercised by a Party Secretary in a High School which functioned as a Secondary Unit of research.

Mary was a music teacher in the High School. She had a private family wedding with the compulsory civil ceremony in January. Her husband is well-known nationally as an artist. A child was born in May. Mary invited some faculty to the baptism of the child in a ceremony at the Romanian Orthodox Church. The Party Secretary reprimanded the faculty who went to the church service. Before the baptism Mary had also announced a church wedding service for June. It is not uncommon in Romania to have separate wedding services, with the church service and reception being the principal social event. Party members and activists are not supposed to attend any church services; if you are a Party member you are not even supposed to have a religious ceremony at your burial, for example.

Mary had invited many faculty members to attend the church wedding which was going to be a big social event in the capital because of the groom's social status as a well-known artist. The Party Secretary forbade the faculty to attend the church service; they should attend only the social function after the religious ceremony. The Party Secretary called a special Party meeting at the school to criticize Mary. The charges brought

against Mary included superstition, negativism,
and fostering a bourgeois spirit in the school.
Five faculty members joined in the criticism of
Mary; one of them proposed an investigation into
Mary's membership in the Party to decide whether
she should be expelled.

Party Secretaries usually do not propose expulsion for periodic attendance at religious ceremonies. In Mary's case, the notoriety of Mary's
husband would mean everyone in the school, including students, would know of the religious
wedding service. Mary's wedding was not only the
practice of bourgeois superstition, but it was also scandal. But in the end, Mary was not expelled
from the Party; her husband's fame had greater influence than the Party Secretary. Mary was only
reprimanded.

Party Secretaries, for example, supervise the
appearance of teachers. In one University department, the Party Secretary did not allow young female faculty to wear make-up. The Party Secretary
herself, because of her dress and excessive use of
make-up was known to students and faculty as the
'hustler of Notre Dame'. In the same University
department, the appearance of the younger female
faculty was expected to be: hair tied back, little
or no make-up, no trousers, skirts to the knee,
stockings and no flamboyant or bright colors.
Males were generally expected to wear a suit and
tie.

The Party Secretary's power base lies in the
ability to criticize faculty or start an investigation because of ideological omissions or errors
on the part of the faculty. Negative entries in
one's dossier can cause difficulty for one's family such as obtaining certain jobs. The Party Secretary also has power in being able to destroy
one's chance of obtaining a tourist visa. When an
individual applies for a passport, or an exit visa
if one already has a passport which is kept by the
police, to travel abroad on a visit, there is an
ideological investigation of the applicant. The

167

Party Secretary at the place of work is asked to report on the ideological behavior of the applicant. A less than positive report from the Party Secretary will result in the refusal of the passport or visa. A report by the Party Secretary is also made when a teacher applies for promotion, a change of position or a change of schools.

It is also the Party Secretary who invites faculty to become members of the Party. Some teachers refuse; but they are in the minority. Refusal is interpreted as antagonism towards the Party; the person invited to be a member who refuses is required to state the reasons for refusal. An invitation to join the Party is officially regarded as a privilege and an honor. The majority of faculty who are members of the Party become members in the early years of their teaching profession. The process of joining the Party, functions as an important part of the ideological training of faculty both for the person invited to join, and for other faculty members.

The person who is invited to join the Party in an educational institution, must have two faculty members of the Party who second the teacher's application to join; the Party members as a group must unanimously agree to the application. If the agreement is not unanimous, the application is postponed. The applicant must state his or her ideological reasons for joining. Then follows the investigation and criticism which may be open or anonymous. The person's school record is checked; an inquiry is made into the ideological training of the faculty member and the degree of political activism; in High School and University, selected students are questioned about the applicant's ideological behavior and suitability as a candidate for membership of the Party. The applicant's family and social history before 1944 is investigated; there is also an investigation into the person's present family, living and social status, and behavior outside the school.

For example, divorce and liaisons must be explained by the applicant, as must not being married, if the applicant is over thirty. If members of the applicant's family, spouse, adult brothers and sisters, parents, are not members of the Party, the applicant must explain the reasons for non-membership. If the applicant has relatives abroad, the applicant must explain why they are abroad and all the circumstances of their position abroad as well as the circumstances of the relationship between the applicant and the relatives. Relationships with all foreigners must be explained. The process of entry into the Party is easier if the candidate is married, has not been divorced, and has at least one legitimate child.

It was explained to me that a person who is single or divorced is more suspect than a married person because he or she may be a homosexual or lesbian; being single is a sign of social irresponsibility in a nation which wants officially to increase its population; but being single also signals instability which can be exploited by outside forces. However, being divorced or single usually does not impede entry into the Party; at worst it postpones entry. But even suspicion of homosexuality or lesbianism will cause expulsion from the teaching profession.

All faculty members can be involved in the criticism and investigation, on the orders of the Party Secretary.

If evidence of ideologically incorrect behavior in the applicant's past is discovered, the application is postponed or rejected, depending on the gravity of the behavior. Usually during the criticism, there is a tacit agreement about not touching on areas of material welfare. Many High School teachers and University faculty, supplement their income by private tuition; sometimes the supplement can more than double one's income giving a very high material standard of living. Engaging in private enterprise of any kind is illegal; one can register with the government as a private tutor and pay tax. The stipend per hour is fixed at a low sum but the normal price for private is between five and fifteen times the fixed rate. Private income and material standard of living is the tacit area of investigation and criticism. In general, in Romanian society, public criticism of the high standard of living of certain groups in society is taboo.

During the process of investigation and criticism of an applicant for entry into the Party, other faculty members may also be criticized for omissions or negativism in their behavior. The Party meeting itself constitutes an important part of the ideological training of teachers.

The Party meeting in general has two sections, criticism and a lecture. There are two kinds of criticism, self-criticism and criticism of others. Periodically, every member is expected to criticize himself or herself. The self-criticism is usually an accusation of not being enthusiastic or an accusation in anticipation of expected criticism from others. Criticism by others is usually confined to areas of omission or, in general, mild criticism. A more serious criticism such as fostering disrespect for the Party is usually a sign of a proposed putsch of some kind. For example, a group of faculty in a University department wanted to get rid of their Party Secretary because of the severity of her criticism and the length and frequency of Party meetings. The Party Secretary was accused of bringing the Party into disrepute because of her rudeness and autocracy with students. Lines were drawn within the faculty between the groups supporting and opposing the Party Secretary. Peace was made by the department chairman when the criticism began to enter the area of life-style and material possessions.

At the Party meeting there is also an instructional period. Faculty are required to study, for example, a recent speech of the President. There is a lecture on the material of the speech, by a faculty member or an outside expert; then the faculty are questioned on their knowledge of the speech. The Party Secretary usually finishes the lecture and question session by outlining what should be done to incorporate the material of the speech or some other material from the propaganda section of the Central Committee, into the teaching or organizational life of the institution.

The instructional period at the Party meeting ensures that all faculty members are kept up to date with the decisions and wishes of the Central Committee. The Party meeting is chaired by the Party Secretary; the Director of the school is present only as a member of the Party. Theoretically, the Party Secretary is in charge of the weekly Party meeting and all matters in the school dealing with ideological instruction, training, and behavior.

All teachers whether members of the Party or not, must attend the weekly meeting of the Teacher's Union. The Union, as officially a front organization of the Communist Party, has a study and instructional section similar to the Party meeting. Sometimes the instruction at the Party meeting has a lecture cycle, over and above the section on the examination of some current item; the instruction at the Union meeting deals usually with current affairs and items such as the recent speeches of the President. The Secretary of the Teacher's Union in the school chairs the Union meetings; the secretary is responsible for giving or delegating the ideological instruction.

At Party and Union meetings, the Party and the Secretary of the Union respectively, frequently delegate the instructional responsibility to another faculty member. At a Union meeting, for example, a faculty member who is not a member of the Party, may have to give the ideological instruction; in the school which was the Focal Unit of research for the High School level, non-Party members of the faculty were, in general, responsible for ideological instruction at Union meetings. The function of a Trade Union in Romania does not

171

include acting as mediator with management on behalf of the employees. In meetings of the Unions
of teaching faculty, the primary item on the agenda is instruction; sometimes there is a discussion
of working conditions such as the cleanliness of
classrooms and blackboards, and the availability
of text-books and audio-visual materials. But
discussions on matters such as the availability of
teaching materials also take place at faculty
meetings. Changes in the labor code, exhortations
from high officials about the importance of work
are usually discussed at Union meetings rather
than at Party meetings. But work-related subjects
are also discussed at Faculty and Party meetings.

But for the most part, the instruction at
Party meetings is duplicated at Union meetings.
The significant difference between Union and Par-
ty meetings is that all faculty are present at
Union meetings, whereas only Party members are
present at Party meetings.

Faculty meetings deal in general with the
academic life of the institution. But in general,
there is some ideological instruction at faculty
meetings also. The amount of ideological instruction at faculty meetings depends upon the political activism of the Director. If the Party Secretary in an institution holds a dominant position
in the institution and is not, in practice, subject to the Director, then the amount of ideological input at the faculty meeting will be in direct
proportion to the Party Secretary's dominance in
the institution.

While ideological criticism is theoretically
confined to meetings of the Party, there is also
some criticism at Faculty and Union meetings, but
more especially at Union meetings.

CHAPTER VII

IDEOLOGY AND IDEOLOGICAL TRAINING: CONCLUSIONS

Can the source of the ideological training be identified? Is there an evolution in the ideological training in the school system in Romania? Is the mode of the training more significant than the content of the training? Is there a unifying factor in the ideology propagated in Romanian schools?

Part I of this chapter will deal with the ideological training: with the source, content, mode, and target of the training. In Part II, I shall attempt to delineate the boundaries of the ideology itself.

Part I: The Ideological Training
Section 1: The Source

The source of the training is multiple, but there is a hierarchy within the multiple source system, with a principal source and intermediate sources. Faculty serve as the immediate source in the training of students in the lower echelons of the school system; in the higher echelons, especially on the University level, student activists and faculty serve as the immediate source in the ideological training of students. Student activists and the faculty at large, are trained by selected faculty such as the Executive Committee of the Communist Party within an institution. The Party Secretary within an institution serves as the immediate source of training for the Executive Committee of the institution.

The Party Secretary of an institution belongs to the lowest echelon of the activist pyramid of the Communist Party structure. The Party Secretary in the Kindergarten, Grade School, and High School has the Executive Committee of the Party on the district level, as his or her immediate source of ideological training. The Secretary of the Executive Committee of the Party on the district level, has the Executive Committee of the Party on the county level as his or her immediate source. The Secretary of the Executive Commiteee of the Party on the county level, and the Secretary of the Party in a University Department or Faculty, have as their source the secretariat of the Central Committee of the Communist Party responsible for propaganda and ideological training.

The secretariat responsible for ideological training and propaganda is governed by the Central Committee. The following diagram illustrates the hierarchy of organs within the Central Committee; the secretariat does not function as part of the Central Committee but as an arm of this apex of the Party pyramid.

The General Secretary	
The Permanent Praesidium	The
The Central Committee Secretariat	Central
The Executive Committee of the Romanian Communist Party	Committee

During the period of my research, the General Secretary of the Party was Nicolae Ceausescu; he is a member of all the major organs of the Central Committee. As President of the country, Ceausescu is also the Head of State. Nicolae Ceausescu's early career had been almost always as a member of the Party apparat; at various times he was directly responsible for the ideological training of youth and the military. As a member of the apparat throughout his career, he has always been involved in political or Party duties, never in purely government or State affairs until he became the Head of State. When he was deputy minister of agriculture in the early '50's, his task was primarily ideological; to convert the peasants to nationalization and collectivization of the land. He is now also the Party's chief ideologue as well as being the undisputed leader of the Party and Head of State.

174

Nicolae Ceausescu is not only the principal source of ideological training in the Romanian school system; he himself, his actions, his ideas, his personality, also forms part of the content of the ideological training. He is the primary source of the ideology both in content, and mode of training. He has stated that the ideas of classical Marxism and Leninism must be understood in the light of contemporary conditions; his speeches serve not only as the contemporary reinterpretation of the classical ideas but also as original development.

The range of Nicolae Ceausescu as the primary, authoratative and infallible source of ideology is wide-ranging. It covers such things as music, writing, the arts, education, the economy, services; but also, for example, such things as increasing the population with the consequent banning of contraceptive devices, abortion, the awarding of special honors with the title of Mother Heroine to women who have large numbers of children, and making divorce both expensive and difficult to obtain. In general, as the principal source of ideology he teaches three principles.

(1) A person should not pursue individual pleasure, or engage in actions for selfish reasons.

(2) All behavior should serve the Party and the State.

(3) The serving of the Party and State should be a consequence of a positive internalized attitude towards and enthusiasm for, serving the Party and the State.

For example: a person should recreate himself in his or her leisure time in such a manner as to return to work better equipped to serve the State and the Party. Everything in the living situation of a person must serve one end, in the creation of Socialism in Romania on the road towards Communism.

Section 2: The Content and Mode of the Training

I have tried in Chapters IV-VI and in more general terms in the latter half of the previous section, to outline the content of the ideological training.

In this section, I want to consider the evolution in the content of the ideological training. I also want to consider the mode of the training and to consider the question of whether the mode of the training is more significant than the content of the training.

The mode of the training can be considered in two ways, one concrete and illustrative, the other more abstract. In Chapters IV-VI, we have seen in detail the concrete mode of the training: through verbalization such as in lectures, and reading and writing; through song and dance; through organizational frameworks such as the Pioneers, the Union of Communist Youth, and the Communist Party; through work engagements, in patriotic, practical and productive work.

Here I want to consider the mode of the ideological training more abstractly, dividing the mode into:

A. Direct OR Indirect

B. Verbal OR Non-Verbal

The difference between direct (Dir) and indirect (Ind) can be illustrated as follows. When a teacher teaches an item in ideology in class, that is direct. When students wave Romanian flags in school as part of a class exercise that is indirect. Verbal (Ver) is using words: Non-Verbal (NVer) is when the training, for example is through work or engaging in the activities of an official organization in the school which has as its purpose, ideological training. The mode of training for a particular ideological item may be:

C. Dir + Ver

For example: a teacher reads a decree of the Central Committee from the newspaper to the students.

D. Dir + NVer

For example: a student has to attend a meeting of the UCY at the University.

E. Ind + Ver

For example: a teacher tells the students in the eighth grade that if they do not get better grades, they will not get into the academic High School and will have to work in a factory.

F. Ind + NVer

For example: a student receives an academic award because of his or her political activism.

G. Positive OR Negative

(A), and (B) refer to mode; (G) refers to content.

Positive (Pos), refers to an item of the official ideology which is in favor, such as: the Communist Party is the family of all true Romanians who love their country. Negative (Neg), refers to an item alien to the official ideology such as westernism in attitude or dress.

Combining (A), (B), and (G) by taking one item from each of the three lines, gives a combination of eight types of ideological training. A type cannot be other than: (Direct or Indirect) + (Verbal or Non-Verbal) + (Positive or Negative). A type cannot exclude a line entry and cannot include two items from the same line.

An item in the ideological training will be categorized as belonging to one of the following

177

eight types:

1. + Dir Ver Pos
2. + Dir Ver Neg
3. + Dir NVer Pos
4. + Dir NVer Neg
5. + Ind Ver Pos
6. + Ind Ver Neg
7. + Ind NVer Pos
8. + Ind NVer Neg

The purpose of using this typology of items in the ideological training is twofold. Firstly, it introduces order into the review of the mode and content of the ideological training. Secondly, different stages in the ideological training can be distinguished by reference to the typology, thus serving as a check for possible different stages, and evolution in the training.

Two types may be manifested at the same time. For example, the children in the Kindergarten may be reciting a poem in praise of the Party; this will be type one (+ Dir Ver Pos). They may also while reciting the poem wave Romanian flags; this will be type seven (+ Ind NVer Pos).

The principal types of training found in each educational institution is as follows:

Kindergarten: (1), (7).

Grade School:
    Grades I-IV: (1), (7).
    Grades V-VIII: (1), (3), (7).

High School: (1), (2), (3), (4), (6), (7), (8).

University: (1), (2), (3), (4), (6), (7), (8).

In the Kindergarten and Grade School there is an emphasis mainly on the positive aspects of the ideology. Individual students are rewarded for

178

their response to the training. In K-Grade IV, the training is based on affect. It is only in Grades V-VIII, that role aspects enter the training, when the students join their first organization which is an official front for the Communist Party. The training in Kindergarten and Grade School is always (+ Pos); it is either (+ Dir Ver), or (+ Ind NVer). The introduction of the Pioneers in Grades V-VIII, introduces type 3, (+ Dir NVer Pos). Organizational life, through membership of the Communist Party or some front organization, continues in Romania until retirement from the work force. It is through membership in the organization of the Pioneers that students start participating in the political life of the society outside the school, in obligatory role activities.

The period of the introduction of role obligations in the ideological training would constitute an important factor in the formulation of hypotheses with regard to the reaction of students to the ideological training. Students in Grade V-VIII have also already acquired a conceptual maturity which enables them to be aware of reactions to the ideology in the adult community. I did not do any formal testing of reaction to the ideology for this age group. But through observation and interview of students, faculty, and parents, I would suggest the following pattern of reaction in the formulation and testing of potential hypotheses. In K-Grade IV, students react positively to the training, which has for the most part an affect basis. With the introduction of role obligations and control of behavior, the students in Grades V-VIII who are already aged 10-14, begin to distinguish two existences, with two different types of behavior: one, in the institution of the school, and the second, in their family and social life. It is during the period of Grades V-VIII that students learn what can be said and done with impunity in school. For example: the President is presented as a hero and leader in school; the students at this age level hear their parent's reactions to the President at home where the President is often addressed in a less than complimentary

179

manner. I have heard adult family members, directly instruct children in what not to repeat
outside the home. I have heard students in Grades
V-VIII tell jokes in the playground about high
Party officials, which were not only insulting but
highly obscene.

Hypotheses dealing with reactions of students
to the ideological training would have to explain
how students learn what is taboo in school. I
would suggest that family and peer influence are
key factors in accounting for the two existences
or modes of behavior.

In the High School there is added new types
of training. For the first time negativism is
directly introduced. Type 2, (+ Dir Ver Neg),
covers such things as attacks on ideas, attitudes,
values, and behavior, which are contrary to the
official ideology. The control of appearance and
life-style is often strictly enforced in the institution, (Type 4: + Dir NVer Neg). The role obligations through organizations and work engagements increase in High School and especially in
University. Testing in Type 1, (+ Dir Ver Pos),
becomes an important factor in entering the University. In University, ideological training
through military service, organizations, work en-
gagemtents, formal classes, and attendance at cultural events and demonstrations, constitutes 30%-
45% of the student's total training.

Students can begin to be political activists
in the High School; but it is in the University
that the relationship between activism and awards,
benefits, and future career can be more clearly
seen. It is also in the University that students
are for the first time directly exposed to the
process and the possibility of joining the Communist Party. The student in the University decides
whether his or her future career will be in the
Party, in the government structure, or in the general category. The University functions as the
first training ground for the official cadre of
the Communist Party Pyramid. But all students in

the University are made aware of the process of political activism. Students who do not engage in political activism observe the behavior of their colleagues who do become activists; the activist students use their colleagues as the target for their political activity.

I would suggest as a potential hypothesis, that the mode of the training is more important than the content of the training. Mode is more important than content because the content of the training can change. For example: from 1944-1976, three people have been credited in the ideology as the primary source: Stalin (1944-1953), Gheorghe Gheorghiu-Dej (1953-1965), and Nicolae Ceausescu (1965-   ). I am not suggesting Dej or Ceausescu are Stalins. But each of the three have the common element of serving as primary sources. All mention of Stalin has now disappeared completely; Dej has been seriously condemned by Ceausescu. Stalin, Dej, and Ceausescu became the primary source of the ideology only when they had rendered opposition within the Party ineffective.

Other changes in the content of Romanian ideology include: the directing of patriotism and nationalism away from Russia and the Soviet Union (1944-1960) to Romania (1960-   ); extreme reduction in the criticism of Western nations; the introduction of a law during the period of research itself, compelling people over a certain income to purchase their house or apartment, thus reintroducing the concept of private property.

But more importantly than changes in the content of the ideological training, is the fact that the official ideology is the only possible ideology. All public behavior in non-trust group situations must be in accord with the ideology; behavior contrary to official ideology is sanctioned. There is no choice of content for students; there is no questioning of content. It does not matter what the content is, there can only be one reaction: conformity and obedience. If the official ideology says 'religion is mythology', the Romanian student cannot question this statement in an inquiring fashion. The student's reaction is determined by the mode of the training which demands conformity. The public truth value of certain groups of propositions is determined by the official ideology; all other propositions must either be in conformity with the ideology or at least not contradict it.

For these reasons I suggest that the mode of the training is more important than the content of the training. I would suggest the formulation of hypotheses based on the following: what the ideological training achieves is not belief in a group of propositions; through the training students learn how to behave politically within the social system, either for their own benefit or at least without sanction.

The mode of the training includes asymmetrical instruction with no participation by students except response in conformity with the ideology and obligatory role participation in organizations and work engagements. The mode of the training primarily trains in control. The students learn the expectations required in their public behavior, verbal and otherwise. While the ideological training exhibits some characteristics in common with, for example, training in a dogmatic religion, there are important differences. The primary source in a dogmatic religion is divine; one can opt out of a dogmatic religion without, for example economic sanction. People who enter an environment for training in a dogmatic religion are either people who enter voluntarily, or are from microsocial units such as the family, where the religion is culturally accepted. In the case of the ideological training in Romania there is no voluntary choosing to accept the ideology; neither can one opt out. There is also no evidence to show that the ideology is accepted in macrosocial units such as the family; the evidence of my research would point towards non-acceptance.

While the content of the ideological training

182

determines the particular detail of the behavioral expectation, it is the mode of the training which determines the general nature of the expectation in behavioral reaction: conformity. The mode of the ideological training must also be considered in reference to the target of the ideological training in educational institutions. Both students and faculty are the targets of the training. In the Kindergarten and Grade School, the faculty undergo more training than the students. The continual training, supervision, and control of the faculty would make plausible the formulation of hypotheses such as: the continual training, criticism and control of faculty is caused by the non-acceptance of the ideology by faculty; or, the continual control and supervision of faculty induces in the faculty non-acceptance of the ideology. Within the wider society, it is difficult to name someone who is not controlled, apart from the General Secretary of the Party.

In my assessment of general reaction in Romania to the official ideology various factors must be taken into account. As we have seen in Chapter II, expenditure in Romania in the area of services is extremely low. Legal economic opportunity is limited to salaried employment which is totally determined by the State structure under the control of the Communist Party. Access to consumer goods and services is extremely limited which has created a non-official, illegal system of hidden extra cost, exchange of favors, bartering, and private enterprise.

Rodica is in the XIth grade. She wants a pair of fashionable jeans. They are not for sale in shops. Foreign jeans exist on the black-market; the price is the equivalent of one-to-two weeks salary of a worker. Jeans are also made in Romania but only for export; in this case there comes into play the system of favors, plus cash exchange. Rodica's parents, through a complex set of personal arrangements, may get access to jeans from the factory.

But where does the money come from for the jeans? In the context of education, teachers give private tuition; the illegal income allows teachers to compete favorably in the process of deviant access to services and consumer goods.

The following situation arises: the Party Secretary in a University department has her own car; her husband also has a car. The cost of a car is equal to three-to-four years salary of University faculty. The clothes she wears are usually foreign as is her make-up and the lenses for her spectacles. She also travels to the West on vacation. The Party Secretary in the department criticized students for westernism in their attitudes and appearance; students were also criticized for wanting to go on visits to the West. The Party Secretary gave private tuition to High School students who wanted to enter the department. The students then are exposed to two kinds of training from this Party Secretary: one, official, the other, non-official.

The behavior of Party activists on the student and faculty level, and the content of the ideological instruction are sometimes contradictory. But another important factor in any assessment of the reaction of students to the ideological training is the fact that when the new regime was introduced after World War II, there were as we have seen in Chapter III, only one thousand members of the Communist Party in Romania. There is no evidence since 1944 that would indicate any internal committment in Romanian society to a communist ideology, except those parts of the ideology which are in conformity with traditional Romanian culture.

A detailed study of the reaction to the ideological training in Romania would involve paying close attention to the context of behavior. An initial distinction would have to be made between public, private, and intimate contexts of behavior as determined by trust and non-trust situations. In the context of public behavior, distinctions

184

would have to be made between, for example: public
Party demonstrations and rallies in the presence
of the President; meetings of the Party when there
are present people from the top and bottom levels
of the Party pyramid; meetings of the Party within
an institution. Research into reaction towards
ideology in Romania would in practice involve research into the multiple contexts of behavior.
Assessing reaction could not be achieved by a poll
or a random sample of the population. The ideology is accepted in the sense that people in certain
contexts behave according to the ideology; the
ideology is also not accepted in the sense that in
certain contexts it is totally rejected and scorn-
ed. The research would involve outlining the context of behavior. Any assessment which would not
be defined by its context would be scientifically
suspect, leading to statements such as two distinguished political scientists made in reference to
the Soviet Union:

> But it would be a great mistake to overlook
> the fact that perhaps the great majority of
> Russians accept the ethical validity of their
> ideology. These Russian artists and writers
> who are cited as evidence of alienative ten-
> dencies in the Soviet Union, more often than
> not accept many of the basic premises of the
> regime and its ideology.[1]

In a scientific assessment of the reaction of
Romanian students to the ideology, the ideology
would have to be separated into its individual i-
tems with each item being tested according to a
paradigm that would incorporate the multiple contexts of behavior.

Part II: The Boundaries of the Ideology

I am not considering the ideology diachroni-
cally but only as synchronic with the research period.

An important distinction in the ideology is
between the aspects of the ideology which are part

185

of the traditional culture of Romania and the aspects which were introduced since the advent of a communist government in Romania.

Patriotism and nationalism have been essential aspects of Romanian culture from before the advent of communism. Many of the traditional aspects of patriotism and nationalism have been retained such as the glorification of the nationalist heroes. There has also been an attempt to mould the traditional aspects with the Communist Party; for example the true Communist is the true Romanian. There also is an attempt to see the vestiges of items of the post-1944 ideology, in the traditional culture; an example of this is the picture of the President as the continuation of the tradition of the Romanian Hero-Leader.

In trying to define the official ideology other than nationalism and patriotism which has been introduced since 1944, the most convenient and thorough definition is: anything which is proposed by the ruling Party organs and especially by the President, Nicolae Ceausescu who as leader of the Party, rules the organs of the Party.

While this definition of the ideology does not say anything about the content of the ideology, it is important as the definition of the essential boundary of the ideology. A corollary of this definition is that the Communist Party hierarchy is the single unit of control. The leader or apex of the Party pyramid, supplies the input of the content of the ideology; the Party also supplies the output in the form of control. The content may vary; the control remains constant. The latter is an essential part of the ideology: that the content should change and adapt to the changing conditions, is itself part of the ideology.

We have seen in Chapters III-VI many examples of the content of the ideology. The boundaries of the content touch on all observable aspects of life, which includes the linguistic spoken, written, or heard. An example of the last is the law

obliging all citizens to report criticism of the
Party by others.

While the ideology enjoins the internaliza-
tion of the content of the ideology and its enthusiastic externalization in such things as un-
selfish work and political activism, there is no
control of real attitude and motive as there is in
some religious ideologies. There is no God who
knows the most secret thoughts and desires. Ideological 'sins' are measured only by failing to
meet the standards of external behavior.

The civil code does not proscribe fornication
and divorce but people who engage in such things
are criticized in Party meetings. In general, the
ethic of sexual behavior corresponds to the Roman
Catholic rules of behavior; contraceptive devices
and abortion for example are directly proscribed
by law. The general Judaeo-Christian ethic pre-
vails in non-sexual areas. It is wrong to steal,
to lie, to cheat or to take part in any activity
contrary to the constitutional government.

What are the Marxist boundaries of the ideology? Which of Marx's teaching has been disregard-
ed? Marx did not want, for example, the State to
have anything to do with education; marriage was
defined by Marx as legalized prostitution.[2] The
economy has been completely nationalized. The
control of the economy is in the hands of the Party oligarchy. To criticize the nationalization of
the economy or its control of the economy is contrary to the ideology, as is any negative criticism of any item of the official ideology. But
nationalization is a first-order fact and so does
not constitute an item of the ideology. First-
order facts such as the control of the economy by
the Party only become part of the ideology indirectly; criticism of certain first-order facts is
forbidden.

In general, the Marxist continuum of historical evolution is part of the ideology: Feudalism,
Capitalism, Socialism, and Communism. Capitalism

is an anachronism but also class producing and ex-
ploitative. In a Socialist state, there can, by
definition, be no antagonistic divisions between
people, because the class system which is the
cause of antagonism in society has disappeared.
Ideology determines reality.

A Western sociologist would probably say
there is a highly developed class system in Romania. But by the definition of the ideology, there
is no class system; in Socialism there are no
class differences and hence no exploitation. The
ideology then acts on different principles of logic from those which I accept, theoretically. The
ideology determines the principles, not reality.

When I say this I do not imply any criticism
of the ideology. I am simply trying to outline
the principles and logical boundaries of the ideology. To posit the source of truth-value in
ideas, or at least outside any reference to the
material world, is a dominant tradition in Western
thought.

General Leninist principles govern parts of
the ideology in Romania more than Marxist principles, especially the important part of the ideology which outlines the control within a state.

"The Soviet Socialist Democracy is in no way
inconsistent with the rule and dictatorship of one
person: that the will of a class is at times best
realized by a dictator who sometimes will accom-
plish more by himself and is frequently more needed . . . ."[3]

"Morality is that which serves to destroy the
old exploiting society and to unite all the toil-
ers around the proletariat, which is creating a
new Communist society . . . ."[4]

The voice of the dictatorship of the proletariat is the Communist Party; the voice of the
Party is the ruling hierarchy of the Party. But
it is the output of the ideology, the control,

which is dominant, not the input, the various
items of the content.

NOTES

1. Gabriel Almond and G. Bingham Powell Jr.,
   Comparative Politics: a developmental appoach.
   (Boston and Toronto: Little, Brown and Co.,
   1966), p. 278.

2. Karl Marx, On Education, Women and Children.
   trans. Saul K. Padover. (New York: Mc Graw
   Hill, 1975), pp. 37-54.

3. Vladimir Ilich Lenin, Isbranniye Proizvedeniya,
   1923 Edition, Vol. XVII, p. 89. Quoted in:
   David Shub, Lenin (New York: Doubleday & Co.,
   1948), Appendix.

4. Ibid., pp. 321-3. Quoted in: Ibid.

BIBLIOGRAPHY

Almond, Gabriel A., and Bingham Powell, G. Comparative Politics: a Developmental Approach.
Boston & Toronto: Little, Brown and Co., 1966.

Arendt, Hannah. The Origins of Totalitarianism.
New York: Harcourt, Brace, 1957.

Barbulescu, D., et al. File din Istoria U.T.C.
Bucuresti: Editura Politica, 1971.

Basdevant, Denise. Against Tide and Tempest: the
Story of Rumania. New York: Robert Speller &
Sons, 1965.

Becker, Howard S. Sociological Work: Method and
Substance. Paperback ed., 1970; rpt. New Brunswick, N.J.: Transaction Books, 1977.

----, et al. Boys in White: Student Culture in
Medical School. Chicago: The University of
Chicago Press, 1961.

Belen'kii, G. I. "The Role of Literature in the
Labor Education of Pupils," Soviet Education,
18,12 (Oct. 1976), 68-76.

Bereday, George Z. F., and Pennar, Jaan, eds. The
Politics of Soviet Education. New York: Praeger,
1960.

Berezina, G. "A Systematic Approach and Consis-
tency in Party Studies," Soviet Education, 15,1
(Nov. 1972), 41-45.

Bertsch, Gary K. Value Change and Political Community: The Multinational Czechoslovak, Soviet,
and Yugoslav Cases. Beverly Hills and London:
Sage Publications, 1974.

Bishop, Robert. Russia Astride the Balkans. New
York: R. M. BcBride & Company, 1948.

Bova Scoppa, R. Colloqui con Due Dittatori.
Roma: Ruffalo, 1949.

Braham, RAndolph L. Education in the Rumanian
People's Republic. Washington, D.C.: U.S. Department of Health, Education, and Welfare,
1963.

-----. Education in Romania: a Decade of Change.
Washington, C.D.: U.S. Department of Health,
Education, and Welfare, 1972.

Bronfenbrenner, Urie, and Condry, John C., Jr.
Two Worlds of Childhood: U.S. and U.S.S.R. New
York: Russell Sage Foundation, 1970.

Catchlove, Donald. Romania's Ceausescu. Tun-
bridge Wells, Kent: Abacus Press, 1972.

Ceausescu, Nicolae. Romania: a Report. Bucharest:
Meridiane, 1972.

-----. Report to the XIth Congress of the Romanian
Communist Party. Bucharest: Meridiane Publishing House, 1974.

Cioranesco, Georges. Aspects des relations
sovieto-roumaines, 1967-71. Paris: Minard, 1971.

Constantinescu, Miron, et al. Istoria Romaniei.
Bucuresti: Editura Didactica, 1969.

Cretzianu, Alexandru, et al. Captive Rumania: a
Decade of Soviet Rule. New York: Praeger, 1956.

Davis, Brian. Social Control and Education.
London: Methuen, 1976.

Dekkers, Rene, et al. Le regime et les institutions de la Roumanie. Bruxelles: Universite
Libre de Bruxelles, 1966.

Deutscher, I. Stalin: a Political Biography. 2nd
ed., 1949; rpt. London, New York: Oxford University Press, 1967.

192

Dissesco, C. B. Les Origines du droit Roumain. Paris: Typographie Chanerot et Renouard, 1889.

Djilas, Milovan. The New Class; an Analysis of the Communist System. New York: Praeger, 1957.

-----. Conversations with Stalin. New York: Harcourt, Brace, & World, 1962.

-----. The Unperfect Society: beyond the New Class. New York: Harcourt, Brace, & World, 1969.

Douglas, Jack D. et al. Existential Sociology. New York: CAmbridge University Press, 1977.

----, ed. Understanding Everyday Life. London: Routledge & Kegan Pual, 1971.

East, W. G. The Union of Moldavia and Wallachia, 1859. Cambridge: Cambridge University Press, 1929.

Education in the Socialist Republic of Romania. Bucharest: Ministry of Education, 1973.

Eidelberg, Philip Gabriel. The Great Rumanian Peasant Revolt of 1907. Leiden: Brill, 1974.

L'Epoque Phanariote. Thessaloniki: Institute for Balkan Studies, 1974.

Evans, Ifor L. The Agrarian Revolution in Rumania. London: Cambridge University Press, 1924.

Fainsod, Merle. How Russia is Ruled. 2nd ed., 1957; rpt. Cambridge, Mass.: Harvard University Press, 1963.

Fischer-Galati, Stephen A. The New Rumania: From People's Democracy to Socialist Republic. Cambridge, Mass.: The M.I.T. Press, 1967.

-----. Romania. New York: Praeger, 1957.

----. The Socialist Republic of Romania. Balti-
more: The Johns Hopkins Press, 1969.

----. Twentieth Century Rumania. New York &
London: Columbia University Press, 1970.

Fischer, George, and Schenkel, Walter. Social
Structure and Social Change in Eastern Europe.
ERIC: Report No. O-PUB-15, 1968.

Fiszman, Joseph R. Teachers in Poland as Trans-
mitters of Socio-Political Values. Washington,
D.C.: Department of Health, Education, and
Welfare, 1969.

Fleron, Frederic J. Communist Studies and the
Social Sciences. Chicago: Rand McNally, 1969.

Florescu, Radu, & McNally, Raymond T. Dracula: a
Biography of Vlad the Impaler. New York: Hawthorn Books, Inc., 1973.

Floyd, David. Rumania: Russia's Dissident Ally.
New York: Praeger, 1965.

Fotino, Georges. Contribution a l'etude des
origines de l'ancien droit coutumier Roumain.
Paris: L. Chauny et L. Quisnac, 1925.

Friedrich, Carl J., and Brzezinski, Zbigniew K.
Totalitarian Dictatorship and Autocracy. Cambridge, Mass.: Harvard University Press, 1956.

Fromm, Eric. The Nature of Man. New York:
Macmillan, 1969.

Georgescu, Vlad. Political Ideas and the En-
lightenment in the Romanian Principalities. New
York: Columbia University Press, 1971.

Ghyka, Matila C. A Documented Chronology of
Roumanian History. trans. Fernard G. Ranier &
Anne Cliff. Oxford: B. H. Blackwell Ltd., 1941.

Giurescu, Constantin. Istoria Romaniei in Data.

Bucuresti: Editura Enciclopedica Romana, 1971.

Gould Lee, Arthur. Crown against Sickle: The
Story of King Michael of Rumania. London:
Hutchinson & Co., (no date).

Grant, Nigel. Society, Schools and Progress in
Eastern Europe. Oxford: Pergamon Press, 1969.

----. "Teacher Training in USSR and Eastern
Europe," Comparative Education, Vol. 8, No. 1
(1972), 7-29.

Greer, Colin. The Great School Legend. New York:
Penguin Books, 1976.

Gulutsan, Metro. "National Identity, Politics and
Education in Romania," Canadian & International
Education, Vol. 1, No. 1 (June 1972), 59-77.

Gurycka A. "Research on Social Passivity of Students", Polish Psychological Bulletin, Vol. 6,
No. 1, (1975), 37-44.

Hale, Julian. Ceausescu's Romania. London:
George C. Harrap & Co. Ltd., 1971.

Hamelet, Michel-P. Nicolae Ceausescu. Paris:
Seghers, 1971.

Harasymiw, Bohdan, ed. Education and the Mass
Media in the Soviet Union and Eastern Europe.
New York: Praeger, 1976.

Honigmann, John J. Culture and Personality. New
York: Harper, 1954.

Ionescu, Ghits. Communism in Romania, 1944-1962.
London, New York: Oxford University Press, 1964.

----. Comparative Communist Politics. London:
Macmillan, 1972.

----. The Politics of the European Communist
States. London: Weidenfeld & Nicolson, 1967.

----. The Reluctant Ally: a Study of Communist
Neo-Colonialism. London: Ampersand, 1965.

Ionescu-Bujor, C. Higher Education in Romania.
Bucharest: Meridiane Publishing House, 1964.

Iorga, Nicolae. Histoire des Roumains. 4 vols.
Bucharest: L'Academie Roumaine, 1920.

----. Histoire des Roumains de Transylvanie et
de Hongrie. Bucharest: Joseph Gobl, 1915.

Johnson, CHalmers, ed. Change in Communist Systems. Stanford, California: Stanford University
Press, 1970.

de Jouvenel, Bertrand. Sovereignty. trans. J. F.
Huntington. Chicago: University of Chicago
Press, 1953.

Jowitt, Kenneth. Revolutionary Breakthroughs and
National Development: the Case of Romania, 1944-
1965. Berkeley: University of California Press,
1971.

Junker, Buford H. Field Work: an Introduction to
the Social Sciences. Chicago: University of
Chicago Press, 1960.

Kassof, Allen, ed. Prospects for Soviet Society.
New York: Praeger, 1968.

----. "The Administered Society: Totalitarianism
without terror," World Politics, No. 16 (July
1964), 558-575.

Kessen, William, ed. Childhood in China. New
Haven & London: Yale University Press, 1975.

Koestler, Arthur, et al. The God that Failed.
New York: Harper & Row, 1963.

Kulich, Jindra. "Training of Cultural Workers,
Political Educators, and Adult Educators in Romania," Adult Education, 49, 1(May 1976), 34-7.

Kuzmin, A., et al. "The Communist Party and
  Ideological Indoctrination," Soviet Education,
  18,6 (April 1976), 3-89.

Laski, Harold J. A Grammar of Politics. London:
  George Allen and Unwin, 1934.

Lodge, Milton C. Soviet Elite Attitudes since
  Stalin. Columbus, Ohio: Charles E. Merrill
  Publishing Co., 1969.

Malinowski, B. "The Problem of meaning in primi-
  tive languages," in Ogden, C. K., and Richards,
  I. A. The Meaning of Meaning. London: Routledge
  & Kegan Paul, 1923.

Manolache, A. General Education in Romania.
  Bucharest: Meridiane Publishing House, 1965.

Markham, Reuben H. Rumania under the Soviet Yoke.
  Boston: Meador Publishing Company, 1949.

Mastny, Bojtech, ed. East European Dissent: Volume 1, 1953-64. New York: Facts on File, Inc.,
  1972.

----. East European Dissent: Volume 2, 1965-70.
  New York: Facts on File, Inc., 1972.

Matley, Ian M. Romania: a Profile. New York:
  Praeger, 1970.

Mead, Margaret. "National Character," in Kroeber,
  A.L., ed. Anthropology Today. Chicago: University of Chicago Press, 1953.

Montias, John Michael. Economic Development in
  Communist Rumania. Cambridge, Mass.: The M.I.T.
  Press, 1967.

Morariu, Tiberiu, et al. The Geography of Romania.
  Bucharest: Meridiane Publishing House, 1969.

Le mouvement educatif dans la Republique Socialiste de Roumanie, pendant l'annee scolaire 1967-

197

1968. Bucharest: Editions Didactique et Pedagogique, 1968.

Muster, Dumitru, and Vaideanu, Gheorghe. "Romania: Contemporary Romanian Education," Journal
of Education, Vol. 152 (February 1970), 64-71.

National Symposium: Psycho-pedagogical Bases of
The Pioneers' Activities. Bucharest, 23-24 May,
1969.

Netea, Vasile. The Union of Transylvania with
Romania. Bucharest: Meridiane Publishing House,
1968.

Newens, Stan, ed. Nicolae Ceausescu. London:
Spokesman Books, 1972.

Oldson, William O. The Historical and Nationalistic Thought of Nicolae Iorga. New York:
Columbia University Press, 1973.

Patrascanu, Lucretiu. Sub Trei Dictaturi.
Bucuresti: Forum, 1942.

The Perversion of Education in Romania. Washington D.C.: Rumanian National Committee, 1950.

Poncet, Jean. Le sous-development vaincu? La
lutte pur le development en Italie meridionelle,
en Tunisie et en Roumanie. Paris: Editions
Sociales, 1970.

Popovici, Andrei. The Political Status of Bessarabia. Washington: Ransdell Inc. for Georgetown
University, 1931.

Popper, Karl. The Open Society and its Enemies.
London: Kegan Paul, 1945.

Ratiu, Ion. Contemporary Romania. Richmond,
England: Foreign Affairs Publishing Co. Ltd.,
1975.

Rey, Violette. La Roumanie: essai d'analyse

regionale. Paris: Societe d'edition d'enseigne-
ment superieur, 1975.

Riker, T. W. The Making of Roumania. London:
Oxford University Press, 1931.

"The Rock Bottom Foundation," Soviet Education, 7,
6-7 (April-May 1970), 51-54.

Roller, Mihail, ed. Rascoala Taranilor. 3 vols.
Bucuresti: Editura de Stat, 1948-49.

Romania's Younger Generation. 2nd ed.; rpt. Bucharest: Meridiane Publishing House, 1974.

Romania's Youth. Bucharest: Meridiane Publishing
House, 1971.

Ronnett, Alexander E. Romanian Nationalism: the
legionary movement. trans. Vasile C. Barsan.
Chicago: Loyola University Press, 1974.

Roucek, Joseph S. Contemporary Roumania and her
Problems: a study in Modern Nationalism. Stanford, California: Stanford University Press,
1932.

---- and Lottich, Kenneth V. Behind the Iron Curtain. Caldwell, Idaho: The Caxton Printers,
Ltd., 1964.

Romania 1959. Bucharest: Foreign Languages Publishing House, 1959.

Romania 1966. Bucharest: Meridiane Publishing
House, 1966.

Romania 1971. 2nd ed. Bucharest: Meridiane Publishing House, 1971.

Romania: Yearbook, 1975. Bucharest: Editura
stintifica et enciclopedica, 1975.

Rura, Michael J. Reinterpretation of History as a
Method of Furthering Communism in Rumania.

Washington, D.C.: Georgetown University Press, 1961.

Sartre, Jean-Paul. Being and Nothingness. trans. Hazel E. Barnes. New York: Philosophical Library, 1956.

----. Critique de la raison dialectique. Paris: Gallimard, 1960.

"The Scientific-Technological Revolution and the Formation of the New Man," Soviet Education, 18, 8 (June 1976), 5-103.

Seisanu, Romulus. Rumania. Bucharest: Imprimeria Nationala, 1939.

Seton-Watson, Hugh. Eastern Europe between the Wars, 1918-1941. Cambridge: Cambridge University Press, 1945.

----. The East European Revolution. London: Methuen & Co., 1950.

Seton-Watson, R. W. Roumania and the Great War. London: Constable and Co. Ltd., 1915.

----. A History of the Roumanians. Cambridge: Cambridge University Press, 1934.

Spigler, Iancu. Economic Reform in Romanian Industry. London, New York: Oxford University Press, 1973.

de Szasz, Zsombor. The Minorities in Transylvania. London: The Richards Press, 1927.

Triska, Jan, ed. Constitutions of Communist Party-States. Stanford, California: Stanford University Press, 1968.

Trond, Gilberg. Modernization in Romania since World War II. New York: Praeger, 1975.

Tufescu, Victor, et al. La Roumanie economique et

culturelle. Geneve: Droz, 1970.

Turnock, David. An Economic Geography of Romania.
London: Bell, 1974.

Upson-Clark, Charles. United Roumania. New York:
Dodd, Mead & Company, 1932.

Vago, Bela. The Shadow of the Swastika. Farnborough, Hants: Saxon House, 1975.

Volounikova, G. M. "Theoretical Problems of
Aesthetic Education in the Study of Literature,"
Soviet Education, 18, 12 (October 1976), 50-67.

Vulpe, Radu. La Dobroudja a travers les Siecles.
Bucharest: Dacia, 1939.

Wallace, Anthony F. C. Culture and Personality.
New York: Random House, 1970.

Wolfe, Bertram D. Six Keys to the Soviet System.
Boston: The Beacon Press, 1956.

Xenopol, Alexandru D. Istoria Romanilor din Dacia
Traiana. 3 vols. Iasi: Saraga, 1896.

Periodicals, Magazines, and Newspapers

Arici Pogonici
Cravata Rosie
Forum
Gazeta Invatamintului
Lupta de Clasa
Revista de Pedagogie
Scinteia
Scinteia Tineretului
The Romanian Bulletin
The Romanian Review
Viata Studenteasca